ASSET SECURITY SYSTEM

BY

JOHN V. CHILDERS, JR., J.D.

ASSOCIATE TAX AUTHOR, JOHNNY TOLLETT, C.P.A.

*To the two lovely ladies
in my life:
my wife, Jill and my daughter,
Mary Katherine*

ACKNOWLEDGEMENTS

W riting a book requires a great deal of time, effort, and energy. While I would like to say I was able to do it all myself, that is simply not the case. Without the tremendous support from those around me this book would not be in your hands right now. I must first thank my good friend and outstanding tax accountant, Johnny Tollett, as he supplied an immense amount of tax examples, wit, and wisdom in making this book a reality. I must also thank his wife, Amber, also a CPA (what a wonderful homelife that must be!), for taking the time to proof-read and constructively criticize our efforts. Next, I need to thank my executive assistant, Michele Hunter, for her long hours of typing, retyping, and putting up with my continuous ranting, raving, changing and then changing back. This book would not have been possible without her efforts and I appreciate them.

Of course I must thank the two people who taught me life's lessons, and then gave me the courage and the chances to make my own way, my parents, John and Brenda Childers. Their continued advice and support are welcomed and appreciated.

Finally, I must thank my wife, Jill and my daughter, Mary Katherine for understanding when I was unable to be home while writing this book and working to build a company. Without their support nothing would be possible.

THE SECRET MILLIONAIRE ASSET SECURITY SYSTEM

TABLE OF CONTENTS

THE SECRET MILLIONAIRE ASSET SECURITY SYSTEM

CHAPTER HIGHLIGHTS

"To escape criticism, do nothing, say nothing, be nothing."
Elbert Hubbard

PREFACE

I t is no secret that millionaires get different results than most people. The trick is to find out what their secret is. What is it that millionaires do to get the type of different results that they get? Do you suppose that they do things the same old way that we've always been taught to do things or do you suppose that they do things differently? The millionaire's secret is that they do things a little differently. As F. Scott Fitzgerald wrote, "The rich are different." While this may not be exactly what he meant, this is certainly true for Secret Millionaires. For our purposes, we mean that they know things that most people do not.

It seems that this would be common sense. Think about it. If you want to get different results you must do things differently. It's almost the definition of insanity to continue to do the same things in the same way but expect to get different results. If you want to build a house, you follow the blueprints to build that house. Too many times, people follow the blueprints to build a cottage while expecting to see a mansion as the end result. It's not going to happen.

When we look at it this way, it would seem ridiculous to think that we could get the results that we really want while doing

> *To achieve the results of millionaires, you must do what millionaires do.*

things the same way we've always been taught to do them. Unfortunately, people simply don't get it. To achieve the results of millionaires, you must *do* what millionaires do.

Why is it that most people fail to accomplish all that which millionaires accomplish? It is because they fail to do those things which millionaires do. They tend to do things the same way rather than differently. The reason for this is that far too often, people are unjustly criticized when trying to do things differently. People find themselves in situations where people laugh at or ridicule them about their dreams. Millionaires did not become that way by listening to this type of criticism.

We all know people who always seem to be able to show you exactly how something won't work. Think about it, do most of the people you know encourage you to be phenomenally successful, or do they seem to influence you into settling for mediocrity? The biggest problem is that the influence that these people have on others is enormous.

If you want to achieve the results of millionaires, you must do what it takes to overcome this negative influence. In deciding to write this book, I was questioned by many as to why I would do it. There were people who wondered why I would write a book on strategies for protecting assets when there are already books on that topic in the bookstores. Others wanted to know whether I thought I was enough of an expert on the topic to be writing this book. Surely there are others out there with more experience or more knowledge. Bottom line, they seemed to be telling me all of the reasons that I should be thinking about as to why I shouldn't do it rather than encouraging me to do it. Believe me, it would have been very easy to simply give up. It would have been much easier to take their advice.

The problem is, like many of you reading this book right now I wanted to be different. I wanted to achieve different types of results. Because of this, I

decided to risk criticism and do something. Naturally, there are those rare individuals who actually commend someone for doing things differently and I appreciate them more than they know. By writing this book, I want to encourage others to be the type of person that makes things happen rather than sitting back and explaining why things won't happen. This book is for those of you who want, no, *demand*, extraordinary results, *different* results.

I explain this to you not to boast about myself, but to prepare you for what you will encounter. By implementing strategies and tools utilized by some of the wealthiest individuals in our country, you will not be doing things in the ordinary way. As such, you will encounter criticism and discouragement. You must persevere and understand that you are doing what it takes to succeed. You are *acting* rather than sitting back and *reacting*. I commend you on that decision and the decision to preserve your family's wealth through learning the infor-

> *You are acting rather than sitting back and reacting.*

mation contained in this book. But you need to be aware that many people will try to tell you to do things the standard way and not to do things differently. In order to explain why you are doing things in a particular manner, you need to be the first to understand it.

This book, *Secret Millionaire Asset Security System*, explains how you too can do those things which many of today's most successful individuals are doing. This book is about implementing dynamic strategies which will help you accomplish your goals in a more efficient and effective manner. Wealth strategies which will enable you to face not only the financial pitfalls awaiting you in the business world in which we live, but also to enable you to preserve your wealth for your family once you are gone. It is a tool which will enable you to

get those different results. This book helps you to better understand these concepts.

The key to the entire *Secret Millionaire* book series is that it is designed to be different. There is an abundance of books out there which tell you a little bit about what things are, this book series is designed to tell you why you might want to *do* certain things. Specifically, the book series explains why you might want to do things differently. It is designed to teach you how you too can become a "secret millionaire."

What is a "Secret Millionaire"?

But what is a "secret millionaire?" How is a "secret millionaire" different from any other millionaire? This is the thing which we really need to understand. In simple terms, a "secret millionaire" is a millionaire who wants to keep his status. Not just the million dollar net worth status, but also the *secret* status. It is easy enough to understand how someone would want to keep a firm hold on their net worth. This book however, is primarily geared toward those who would not especially like for the whole world to know that their net worth resides in the seven digit plus realm. Is it because they are ashamed of their success? Of course not. It is because we are in the middle of a terrible war right now. A war so dangerous that we must do what it takes to protect ourselves from those who are seeking to destroy us. This book is about how to do just that. If you wish to survive this war, you better be ready for combat. In the words of C.E. Montague, "War hath no fury like a non-combatant." Prepare for battle!

"The future belongs to those who prepare for it."
Emerson

Chapter I
The Secret Millionaire

N ow, more than at any other time in this country, you must become a "secret millionaire." War has been declared on the people of this country and if you are not prepared, it will devour you. To prepare yourself, you must understand the importance and the seriousness of the situation.

Imagine that you are sitting in your living room reading a book one night and you hear a noise outside. It sounds strange and you begin to get a little scared. Maybe it's just your imagination since you're reading the latest thriller by Stephen King. Maybe there really is something out there. You pay close attention but nothing happens.

The sound stops, so you feel safe once again. Perhaps your imagination was simply getting the best of you. But wait, you hear it again and this time you realize that you are certainly not just hearing things, the threat is real because you notice the shadow of someone trying to get into your house. Even worse, it looks like there may be more than one. On top of that, it looks like they may be carrying weapons.

Panic begins to set in. Immediately, you wonder to yourself, "Did I lock the doors? Did I set the alarm? Is my fortress secure? Am I protected? Is my family protected?" The problem is, you don't have locks on your doors and you don't have an alarm. You, or perhaps the members of your family, are

sitting there all alone with no one and nothing to help you. An unfortunate situation is sure to occur and there is nothing to keep it from happening. Your life begins to flash before your eyes. The last thought that pops into your mind before the inevitable happens is: If only I'd done something to prepare for this.

Does this sound pretty grim? Does it scare you to think of yourself involved in a situation such as the one I just described? The problem is, today we are in a situation that can be every bit as devastating. There is an epidemic in this country and one of the chief enemies is the lack of planning, the lack of implementing a proper system for protecting hard-earned assets.

In the world we live in today, people can easily find themselves in a financial and/or legal crisis that can destroy their estates and even their lives in many instances. Taxes and lawsuits can and will take a large chunk of everything that you have worked so hard to accumulate unless you *learn* how to implement an effective asset security system and do what it takes to protect yourself.

> *Taxes and lawsuits can and will take a large chunk of everything that you have worked so hard to accumulate unless you learn how to implement an effective asset security system and do what it takes to protect your self.*

And these are certainly not the only things that can devour finances, destroy estates and ruin all that people have built for themselves, their retirement and for their children. Other forces are at work today which can be every bit as devastating. You need to know what these forces are, and how to overcome them. It was with that thought in mind that this book was written.

What is this book about?

This book is designed to teach you exactly how you can implement an asset security system for protecting your hard-earned assets so that you are protected from the dangerous environment prevalent in today's litigious society. More specifically, this book will introduce and teach you how to understand and use the components which make up the asset security system in order to help not only you, but your family as well.

The material in this book is laid out in a question and answer format so that you can use it as both a guide for planning and also as a general reference source on asset security system components. That way, if you have a particular question about these components, you can thumb right to the answer.

The main thrust of this book is to help you understand exactly what you are dealing with and learn how you can protect yourself. There are a lot of reasons for doing so, and you need to understand them all. Then you can use that information to protect yourself, your family and your estate from potential catastrophic financial loss. Most importantly, by studying this material, you will develop a firm understanding and appreciation for the field of asset protection and understand how to use your asset security system for achieving important family and estate planning goals. As the title implies, you need to be implementing the secrets applied by today's millionaires.

One thing you will notice about the books in the *Secret Millionaire* series is that every book begins with the same information. This is done so that those who have not read one of the other books in the series can understand this important information. However, the most crucial reason for including this

information again is to underscore the importance of it. As such, we will be covering these important areas in this introductory section.

While working with investors, small business owners, and many others over the years, I have constantly encountered those in need of the planning provided through proper implementation of an asset security system. The problem was that these people did not know where to find the necessary information, and even when they did, they could not understand it. This book has been formatted to explain what you need, where to find it, and exactly how the asset security system concept can work for you and your particular situation. And it does it in plain, ordinary language instead of legal jargon. This book will be of great importance to you regardless of your current situation or experience level.

The asset security system is one of the best plans available for accomplishing many of your personal goals, whatever they may be. Most of the concerns people have about their family's financial future fall within three main categories. By focusing your attention on these three areas, you can make a big difference in a place where you would most like to see improvement, your family's financial future!

The first area that you need to look at is asset protection. The second is estate planning and the third is tax reduction, an area of immense interest to just about everyone. These three areas can mean a great deal in accomplishing whatever it is that you want to achieve in your business as well as personal life.

Asset Protection

In the area of asset protection, it is really important for you to understand what a litigious society we live in. That means, in plain language, that a lot of folks are suing a lot of other folks, and often for very frivolous reasons.

The best way to illustrate this is by taking a look at a few key statistics on lawsuits. Actual numbers will usually open your eyes to something that you really need to take to heart. The following statistics should do just that.

Studies show that a new lawsuit is filed in this country every thirty seconds on average. That's two a minute, people! To make this point hit home, think about what that really means. In the short time that it's taken you to read this first chapter, several lawsuits have already been filed somewhere against somebody. Lives have been changed, forever! Financial pictures have been altered, irrevocably. Entire family futures have been put in jeopardy. The worst part of this is that it could often be avoided by taking a few simple steps. But that is just the beginning.

One out of four people will be sued this year in this country. Even worse, the average number of lawsuits over an individual's lifetime is five, and of these five, one will be what is known as a "devastating" lawsuit. The term devastating means that it wipes someone out completely, costing them everything they own. It's a horrible sight to see somebody ruined by this kind of litigation, but it *does* happen. By studying this and other books in the *Secret Millionaire* series carefully, as well as taking advantage of the various educational materials in this program, you can go a long way toward making sure it does *not* happen to you.

As you can begin to see, rampant litigation is a big problem in this country. Everyone needs to learn what can be done to help eliminate this problem. This becomes particularly important when you consider that of all the lawsuits filed in the entire world, ninety-four percent are filed right here in the good old United States. Ninety-four percent! We're the world's leader in filing lawsuits. Now, I don't know about you, but that's not an area I would prefer to lead the world in.

Combine these statistics with the fact that there are currently more law students in law school than there are practicing attorneys and it becomes downright scary, doesn't it? Why is that? Why are law degrees in such high demand these days? Is it because we have a shortage of lawyers in this country? I don't think so!

Flip through your telephone book and see how many attorneys there are in your area alone. There is certainly no lack of membership in the legal profession. The number of lawyers is constantly growing, not because there is a larger need, but because there is more opportunity out there for someone to file and win a lawsuit.

With this in mind, which way do you think the number of lawsuits is going in this country, up or down? Up, up, up, of course! Now more than ever, asset protection needs to become a central concern in your financial planning. You absolutely must have a plan to protect your assets, and the use of legal entities should be an essential element in that plan.

Estate Planning

A consideration of equal importance to asset protection is estate planning. Too many times, families unexpectedly discover that enormous amounts of their wealth are being consumed by estate taxes, fees, and other expenses upon the death of a loved one. The worst part of these tragedies is that many of these situations could have been avoided by implementing simple estate plans using the tools you are learning right now. The use of these tools will be the primary thrust of this book.

Unfortunately, people fail to utilize these tools because they do not believe the tools are necessary. It is sad but true that most people spend more time planning their vacations than they do planning their estates. Studies have

> *It is a well known axiom that if you fail to plan, you plan to fail.*

indicated that the average person will spend over ninety thousand hours working to accumulate wealth (forty hours a week times fifty weeks a year for forty-five years of their working lives), but less than three hours learning how to preserve that wealth. These people simply fail to plan their estates. It is a well known axiom that *if you fail to plan, you plan to fail.*

Part of the reason for this failure to plan is that historically, estate planning has been an area reserved only for the truly wealthy. If your bank account and assets didn't total into the six figure range, at a minimum, the traditional line of thinking was that you need not worry about estate planning. People have had the mind set that if they were not from a family whose last name conveyed enormous wealth, they did not need any estate planning. As you well know, that is certainly not the case anymore. *Everyone needs an estate plan.* You

need to ask yourself a question. Would you like to have the estate plan of the average person, or the estate plan used by many of today's millionaires?

The simple truth is everyone needs to be concerned about estate planning, even if you live from paycheck to paycheck. You are dealing with forces, right now, that can destroy everything you have worked all your life to accumulate. And it can happen in the blink of an eye! The example that I posed at the beginning of the chapter is certainly not farfetched. This is essentially what happens to thousands of people every single day in this country. Throughout this book, I will show you the important information which you must understand in order to protect yourself and your family.

Tax Reduction

The third key area of concern in this book is one which is near and dear to all of our hearts. And that is the area of tax reduction. No matter where I go or whom I talk to, it seems that this area is of primary importance. It sure seems that everyone I speak with says they are paying too much in taxes. And I'm not talking about income taxes alone. There are plenty of taxes in addition to income taxes. One of the taxes which we will be dealing with in this book is the estate tax. Most importantly, we will be dealing with how to *reduce* that estate tax.

The whole topic of tax reduction is one of immense interest to most people. Believe me, I hear it all the time. Whether in a seminar, on an airplane, in my business, or even at church, I hear the same old refrain about how bad a person's tax situation has become. When I hear this story, I always ask the same question: *So what are you doing about it?*

It seems that everyone wants to reduce their tax bill but very few are willing to do what that requires. The simple fact is *you* have got to *learn* to reduce your tax bill. Nobody is going to do it for you. If you doubt me on this, ask yourself a question. When was the last time you got that letter from the Internal Revenue Service (IRS) stating that you could have paid a lot less in taxes if you had done things differently? You see, the IRS will not teach you how to reduce your taxes, you must do it yourself. Nobody cares about reducing your taxes more than you do. Since that's the case, *you* must learn how to do it. It's up to you!

> *The simple fact is you have got to learnto reduce your tax bill.*

Having control over your tax bill can mean a great difference in your life. The hard part in all of this is convincing people that they are indeed in control. It seems too hard a pill to swallow that they may in fact be the problem. It's much easier to blame the problem on someone else.

Think about that for a minute. What have you done this year to reduce your tax bill?

Let me take time out right now to commend you for taking the time out of your schedule to read this book. That's a real step in reducing your taxes both now and later, and nobody made you do it. This information can make a tremendous difference in your financial future, if you will just apply it once you've learned it. To reduce the amount you pay in taxes, you have to *do* something about it.

The key is knowledge. You must accumulate as much knowledge as you can about understanding your tax situation. Read tax newsletters, books, the Tax

Code, IRS Publications, and anything else that you can get your hands on to increase your knowledge base. Go to the bookstores and/or libraries and devour their tax material. Continually gain more and more tax knowledge. This is an investment that can provide exponential returns in the form of increased tax savings. This can result in savings for generations to come as well.

While knowledge is certainly the key, the implementation of that knowledge is the most crucial step. It does you no good whatsoever to learn the information if you fail to do anything with it. The use of a living trust can help you to significantly reduce certain taxes. However, it only works for those who are willing to exert the effort required to implement the strategies. You must take control over your situation or your situation will take control of you.

SUMMARY

The landscape is dangerous out there. A war is taking place which will require a great deal of knowledge and savvy in order to survive. The areas of asset protection, estate planning, and tax reduction must be on your mind constantly if you intend to become a Secret Millionaire. You need to continually build upon your knowledge base and develop a greater understanding of how to best address these concerns. Read this and other books over and over again to familiarize yourself with the contents and implement the information contained herein. There are excellent ways to structure your affairs but the responsibility for their implementation lies with you. *You are in control!*

You are in control!

"What on earth would a man do with himself if something did not stand in his way?"
H.G. Wells

CHAPTER II
SECRET MILLIONAIRE
ASSET PROTECTION

What is asset protection? Why would I need asset protection, I don't break the law? I'm not a criminal and only criminals need to hide their assets! I don't have millions of dollars or anything of immense value worth suing for! I don't have that many debts and the few I do have are manageable! I don't have to worry about asset protection until I make at least two or three times as much money as I currently earn. If I get into a bad situation, then I can just transfer my assets to someone else, right?

I meet many, many people who have these same misconceptions about what asset protection is, who needs it and how you go about establishing an asset protection plan. All of this misunderstanding out there clearly begs the question, "Exactly what is asset protection?"

What is asset protection?

Legal asset protection, simply put, is taking measures that are outlined and allowed by your state and federal government to preserve your wealth from a multitude of dangers. I don't think I have to tell you that we are most certainly a "sue happy" society! No longer are lawsuits only filed against bad people who have done something wrong. We hear about people who file ridiculous

THE SECRET
MILLIONAIRE

lawsuits in the news almost daily. We read in disbelief when someone loses everything they have worked for to a ludicrous claim. We make lawyer and "whiplash" jokes without realizing just how close to the truth we really are.

> *Sometimes it seems that lawsuits are the newest "get rick quick" scheme in America.*

Sometimes it seems that lawsuits are the newest "get rich quick" scheme in America. The sad reality is that if you own anything, what you own is at risk! The American dream is indeed alive and well, but for many it is built on the hard work and misfortune of someone else!

I call this program the *Asset Security System*, because I feel that a security system for your assets is something that most Americans are lacking. We have home and car security systems to protect these assets, we employ security companies to monitor and safeguard our business assets, and we even purchase insurance to protect our interest in the event of a loss. What most people don't do however, is to take the next step to combine these security systems with the legal entity "security systems" which can become a proverbial wealth fortress to protect the things that you have worked so hard to accumulate.

Why is asset protection important?

If you think that these are all scare tactics, let me give you some cold, hard facts, and let me tell you, these are perhaps the most frightening part of all. As I stated in the preface, on average, a new lawsuit is filed every *thirty seconds* in this country! If we take this statistic to its logical conclusion, that's 120 lawsuits an hour and 2,880 new lawsuits filed every day!! To reiterate another point in the preface, one out of every four people will be sued this year

in this country. So on average, each and every person in the U.S. has a 25% chance of being sued this year. What's even more frightening is that if you are married or are otherwise partnered, for example, in a business, the chances of your "partnership" being sued are an average of 25% *for each person in the partnership*! As you can imagine, as more people are encouraged by this trend to continue to try for "easy money," the number of lawsuits will just keep going up.

We know that the college and university programs tend to fluctuate around job demands from the business and employment world. When there is a demand for more employees with training in a particular field, like nursing or computer systems, the salaries in those fields go up to compete for the most skilled, and the college enrollment in those areas jumps as well. Following this trend, there are currently more law students in law school than there are practicing attorneys. Ladies and gentlemen, someone is going to have to pay these future attorneys' salaries. How are they going to make their money? In my opinion, it will be one of two ways. Either by representing those filing all those lawsuits, or by defending those who find themselves the targets of this onslaught of legal hyperactivity.

Who are you protecting your assets from?

Now that you've read the previous paragraphs, I think we should agree that the best definition of the term "asset protection" is that it is a legal form of "self-defense." It is not evading our financial responsibilities or avoiding liability for criminal behavior. There are far too many legal means with which to protect yourself to resort to the illegal ones.

Like the adaptations that animal species must go through in order to survive in constantly changing environments, asset protection is a logical outcome or reaction to the litigious financial environment in which we live. It is a survival of the financial "fittest." Will you and your family become financially extinct, or will you survive the changes in the financial climate and emerge stronger and more vital? If the latter is where you want to be, then you must take the necessary steps to protect what you have worked so hard to build. You are taking the first step right now by reading this book, you are learning *how*. We will teach you the necessary steps, but it is up to you to act.

If the outrageous lawsuits and legions of future attorneys aren't enough to convince you that your assets need protecting, let me mention a few other unexpected and often unforeseen threats to your wealth. If you still believe that lawsuits only happen to "other people," I want to remind you that threats can come from virtually everywhere.

Most of us know or know of someone who has faced this particular scenario. An unexpected and serious illness of themselves or a family member creates astronomical medical bills or loss of income. Even with medical insurance coverage, there are ceilings or maximum amounts that the insurance will pay. There is often a percent or co-pay for which the insured, that's you, is responsible. There may be limitations to your sick leave or disability payments, which mean no income while infirmed. Costly cutting edge or experimental treatments are often cited as being "unnecessary" or "untested" by insurance. And remember that as we live longer and as medicine and the bacteria it fights become more advanced, the chances of our having an expensive medical payment in our lifetime increases.

Another situation which has become more and more prevalent with the cata-

strophic weather disasters of the past several years has been the bankruptcy of insurance companies. Extreme weather and weather related disasters can drain the resources of insurance companies to the point where they literally "break the bank." There simply isn't enough money to pay out to the claimants. Less extreme, but just as damaging to you as an individual is the cancellation of an insurance policy due to a claim, or too many claims. This is common in flood plain areas or even for policyholders who experience house fires. That's right, house fires.

While we are on the topic of insurance, what about an auto accident? Your insurance will cover that, right? What if your accident is with an uninsured motorist (there are still plenty of those out there!) or if the motorist is insured and the damages exceed your policy limits? Who is personally liable for the rest of the damages? Unfortunately, you are. With the cost of automobiles these days, you could be paying tens of thousands of dollars out of your own pocket.

A very serious and very common threat to your wealth that we often don't consider from this perspective is divorce. With divorce rates at 50% and climbing, this is a real issue. In an amicable divorce, an estate may be divided right down the middle. Even in a fair and friendly division this could often mean liquidation of some of your most valuable assets. Think about how easily divorce could decimate your wealth. In an instant your one million dollar estate is chopped into two $500,000 dollar ones, and this is *before* attorneys' fees!!! Think about your current lifestyle. Now think about how drastically your lifestyle would change if the total value of your assets was cut in half! You might be lucky enough to maintain your current status, but how much harder would that become financially?

We've all either experienced the nightmare or heard the stories from those who did, of the dreaded tax audit by your state tax agency or the IRS. Even if you come out of the audit with no additional taxes or penalties, you have had to pay out additional fees for legal or financial professionals to represent you. If you do face a large assessment for taxes, penalties and interest, you are expected to come through with payment forthwith. Unless you can liquidate some assets quickly, and possibly face capital gains next year, you could be handing over your hard earned assets to the tax man. Even if you can "afford" it, who really wants to give the government more than its fair share of what you earn?!

If you own your own business, you already realize that you face a multitude of potential hazards to your wealth and assets. The threats exist, from employee filed claims such as sexual harassment or any number of discrimination suits, to suits for personal injury or property damage from customers, visitors or even trespassers to your establishment, to claims of negligence filed against you for services or employee work not properly performed. Just the image that you have something of value makes you prey for those who want to get rich off your misfortune. Hence, the necessity of becoming a Secret Millionaire is at an all-time high.

The far reaching effects of the bankruptcy of a company's major client are felt by both employer and employee. Layoffs, restructuring and the possibility of the company's own bankruptcy are real threats to your wealth whether you own, or are employed by the company.

You simply must become aware that asset protection is not merely the realm of the ultra-wealthy or the criminal. It is necessary, no, *vital* to your financial

survival.

Who needs to protect their assets?

We have already established the fact that lawsuits are a definite threat to everyone, even you. So the next question is, "Do I have anything to protect?" I make reference to this scenario throughout the book but I believe that it bears repeating. Imagine for a moment that you hired me to come to your home and install a home security system. I examine your house itself, your vehicles, your furniture, your jewelry, your entertainment equipment, and the remainder of your personal possessions. Upon completion of my examination I tell you that you don't need a home security system. I determined essentially, that your stuff was not worth protecting. How would you feel? You would probably be angry and insulted.

Now let's switch roles. You hire me as your attorney and ask me how to best protect the assets you have accumulated. I look at the situation and take you step by step through the maze of legal entities, trusts, and retirement plans. I show you how these entities can help shield your assets from potential creditors. After going over all relevant aspects of your situation, you decide to do nothing because you don't have the time, or you don't want to spend the money. In essence, you have just made the determination that your stuff was not worth protecting. How would you feel now?

The fact is we all have "stuff" worth protecting. Asset protection should be a concern of everyone, not just the wealthy. Remember, asset protection can mean protecting assets you have not even acquired yet, such as future salaries or business interests. At no time in my practice do I see clients get more

passionate and concerned than when we talk about planning for their children's future. This is a concern we all share. Making sure our children have a better chance than we did is a universal mindset. Do you realize that one run stop sign, one sliced tee shot, or even one spilt cup of coffee could jeopardize all that you have worked so hard to accumulate? While asset protection should be at the top of everyone's "to do" list, (actually it should be at the top of the "completed" list) unfortunately this is an area that is drastically overlooked by millions of Americans.

> *Do you realize that one run stop sign, one sliced tee shot, or even one spilt cup of coffee could jeopardize all that youhave worked so hard to accumulate?*

What is involved in the overall asset protection planning process?

Asset protection is an ongoing process. One simple act today will not necessarily solve your problems for the long run. Asset protection must be accomplished in a systematic way with specific goals in mind. I like to play with acronyms. They help me keep in focus what I am trying to accomplish. Basically, asset protection is the process of defending your assets. Therefore, we will use the acronym *DEFEND* to help establish this process.

Define your goals
Engage professional assistance
Forethought
Education
Never stop learning
Decide to implement

Let's take a look at these a little closer.

Define your goals

Before you can implement any strategy, you have to know what you are trying to implement. Thus, you must define your goals. You must know what you wish to accomplish. The first step in asset protection would be to determine what your financial makeup is. These include topics such as:

- What are your sources of income?
- What are your current assets?
- What are your current liabilities?
- What are your estimated future assets?
- What areas of personal liability are you concerned with the most?
- What areas of personal liability have you not thought of yet?
- What assets would you not want to lose in a lawsuit?
- What is your asset protection plan going to accomplish?

Once you have a clear understanding of the many assets you have at risk, you can better understand what type of strategy needs to be put into place.

Engage professional assistance

Once you decide that asset protection is indeed for you, the next step is to find experts in this field. Most assets protection strategies involve very professional and legal concepts that require the use of an attorney, CPA, financial

planner, or all three.

More Americans use CPAs on a routine basis than they do attorneys. Taxes must be filed every year. Tax planning is an ongoing concern. Hence, CPAs are often the first professionals consulted when it comes to a more complex strategy with regards to your financial portfolio. This is where we come to an important distinction between the legal world and the accounting world. You see, accountants have their expertise in taxes or financial statements. They are not involved in the practice of law every day. If you were to ask your CPA, "At what point should I incorporate my small business?" He or she might very well answer, "Once your net income reaches $50,000. Until then, you would not get much of a tax benefit by incorporating." The fact is that this is a very good answer from the tax standpoint. It does not address, however, any legal benefits involved with incorporating. Is incorporating a small business worthwhile if it only protects your home and other personal possessions from potential creditors? It is possible that incorporating a small business may only give minimal tax advantages, however, the legal benefits involved should make incorporating a top priority.

Conversely, not all attorneys are experts on asset protection, either. Sure, they had to memorize small portions of it for a short while when they took the bar exam, but not all attorneys practice in the area of business entities and asset protection. There are divorce attorneys, personal injury attorneys, trial attorneys, and many, many more. Many of these attorneys come into contact with a formation of a corporation or LLC about as often as you do, if not less.

My point here is not to bad-mouth the accounting or legal professions. My point is to make you aware that just because they have a few letters behind

their last name, they are not automatically experts in all fields of business, especially a business concept as critical as asset protection.

This being said, it is important that you seek out professionals who are knowledgeable and experienced in this field. The strategies and plans they can help you implement should be worth far more than the cost of their services. For information on how you can utilize the services of an asset protection specialist, call Profit Publishing Group, Inc. toll-free at 877.868.9742.

Forethought

Never is the phrase "hindsight is 20-20" more applicable than in the area of asset protection. It is easy to realize the value of proper planning once you are involved in a lawsuit. Once an incident occurs and you have been sued, it is too late to re-arrange your affairs to shield your assets from creditors.

A proper asset protection strategy starts with the fundamental belief that you will be sued in your lifetime. The question now is "when"? Approaching your plan with this attitude will make you search for every advantage you can find. Professional football players practice plays and techniques daily that they may never use in games. Their goal is to have enough sound offensive plays and defensive techniques that they feel extremely confident about their ability to compete and win. In the same way, you will feel confident and secure about your asset protection strategy, even if you never have to use it. Oftentimes, would-be creditors will not even challenge you with a frivolous lawsuit once their contingency-fee based attorneys realize the impenetrable defense you have implemented.

It is also important to remember that asset protection involves assets and income you have not even accumulated yet. It is human nature to improve your standard of living as you mature and become older. Salaries tend to go up. Business opportunities are presented to you. Other family members pass on and leave assets to you. There are hundreds of ways for your net worth to increase as you get older. Your family may also increase in size with a marriage or children. My point here is to realize that just because you think you are O.K. now, you may not think that way tomorrow.

This reminds me of an experience I had when purchasing a new vehicle several years ago. Through the process of selecting a vehicle, I spoke with representatives from nearly every automobile manufacturer you can think of searching for the right vehicle to fit my needs and preferences. As you can imagine, the options available and components of each of these cars was rather similar from vehicle to vehicle. The representative who made the greatest mark on me was the one from the Mercedes-Benz dealership. As you can guess, the price for their vehicles was a bit higher than most of the others. I asked him why it should cost that much more for essentially the same options as were available on the other vehicles I'd looked at. His answer made a distinct impression on me and is the reason I go through this story with you now. He said to me, "The reason that this car is so much more than the others is that it comes equipped with options that we sincerely hope you never have to use."

Of course, he was referring to the tremendous safety features which are standard on all of their vehicles. His response certainly made me think. It reminded me of all of the various reasons to set up an asset protection plan. In the event that I actually have to use the safety features, the things I save will be well worth the initial cost. Without the essential safety features, no amount of

money in the entire world can bring those things back.

Education

Education is the process by which you learn and become familiar with a wide variety of asset protection strategies. I often find that people become enthralled with my seminars, audio and video tapes, and books. When I speak to groups of people, I have to set limits on question and answer sessions. You see, people get excited when they are presented ideas and techniques that are cutting edge. They just cannot seem to get enough of it. Ironically, most of these people did not realize the degree to which they would get involved when they started.

Education on topics as complex as these cannot be attained by reading one book, attending one seminar, etc. For instance, this book only covers the very basic asset protection strategies involved with corporations, limited partnerships, limited liability companies, trusts, and retirement plans. It is intended to get you excited and thinking about the many opportunities available to you to help protect yourself and your loved ones. If you think you have all the answers after you have finished this book, think again. This book would serve as step one in your education process.

Education can be attained in many ways. The most obvious is research. However, research on your part involves many hours of wondering where to start or where to go next. The good thing about nerds and bookworms like me is that I have already done some of your research for you. I put on seminars around the country where I teach the complex and cutting edge strategies that are touched on in this book. I have audio and video tapes

which cover these amazing techniques in more detail.

Where do you think I come up with this stuff? They only teach you so much in law school. The truth is, I spend my spare time attending seminars others put on. This is tax deductible, of course. I read books that others have written. I listen and watch other tapes people have made. I constantly strive to remain as current as possible on the strategies that protect our lives. Once you immerse yourself in the strategies outlined in this book, you may well find yourself involved in the same type of quest for knowledge that I am involved in. This becomes increasingly important as you will see with the next point in our asset protection process.

Never stop learning

Education is an on-going process. As mentioned earlier, there is no way to learn all there is to know about asset protection by reading one book or attending one seminar. In the same way, once a strategy is implemented it must be constantly monitored to see if there are better alternatives or if situations have changed. Remember, we are dealing with legal and tax laws. When is the last time that you heard of a law changing? Probably last week. We live in a society that is constantly changing and on the go. Like it or not, we have to stay on top of these changes in order to best secure what we have accumulated for future generations.

Let's say you took your attorney's advice and formed a corporation. You now have begun to implement your asset protection strategy. However, you have only just started to learn all there is to know about corporations. You need to know how they work, how they are taxed, how money goes in, how

money goes out, what forms you have to file, what paperwork is required of you, etc. True learning is realizing there is more you need to know. More knowledge opens more questions. Learning is a never ending process.

> *Learning is a never ending process.*

Decide to implement

The last, and most important, step in the asset protection implementation process is to do it. You can have all of the goals, professional help, forethought, and education you need, but if you haven't decided to start your plan, it does you no good. A judge will not grant you leniency because you were "thinking about incorporating."

Needless to say, if I have not convinced each and every one of you that lawsuits in this country are out of control and are only going to get worse, then I have not adequately done my job. Do you realize that it is more likely for you to be struck by lightning twice during your lifetime than to live your life without being sued? Think about it. The small cost of protecting yourself and your loved ones is definitely worth the comfort and security that implementing these strategies will bring.

When is the best time to begin your asset protection plan?

The answer to this question is simple, yesterday. Another day that you live without having implemented a plan is another day that some unforeseen incident could happen which could destroy your financial future. How many of you drove to work this morning? If you answered "yes" then you are putting

your wealth and future at risk. Insurance will only cover so much. A good insurance policy will pay a maximum of $100,000. Most injury and death claims start at much more than that.

This is not an area of your life in which you want to procrastinate. Next year, next week, or even tomorrow could be too late. Once an incident that sparks a lawsuit occurs, it is too late to implement plans and strategies that will help. Most of the ideas and concepts that are talked about in this book are very affordable, considering the vast amount of benefit they provide.

Remember, asset protection is not just for the wealthy. It is for you. Why do you think wealthy people implement these strategies? It is not solely because they are wealthy. They implement these strategies because they work. Rich people know how to get the most out of their dollars. That is why they will spare no expense to protect the wealth they have worked so hard to achieve. Why should you be any different from them? Remember, to become a Secret Millionaire, you have to think like a Secret Millionaire.

How do I implement an asset protection plan?

Learning about the inner workings of asset protection strategies is an absolute must to becoming a Secret Millionaire. Asset protection is such an integral part of the overall process that you simply cannot leave yourself without the knowledge of how to implement a properly structured plan. Profit Publishing Group, Inc. has developed books, audio and video tapes, software, and educational seminars designed to help you gain the necessary understanding of the area of asset protection. Not only that, they also assist individuals with formulating and establishing a custom tailored asset protec-

tion plan as well. If you are ready to take control of your finances, call toll-free at 877.868.9742. Call today!

"The greater the obstacle, the more glory in overcoming it."
Moliere

CHAPTER III
SECRET MILLIONAIRE
ESTATE PLANNING

O ne of the greatest obstacles to preserving wealth is the government's relentless attack on wealth passed from one generation to the next. This is a major hurdle which must be overcome in order to have all that you've worked so hard to acquire be distributed in the way that you wish. The government, along with the various laws it has passed to govern the distribution of wealth, poses the single greatest threat to your heirs. This makes it all the sweeter when you learn the closely guarded secrets of the ultra-wealthy and implement those into a well-structured estate plan.

In this chapter, we will be delving into the topic of estate planning and providing you with the basic concepts upon which your overall estate plan will be built. In structuring your Secret Millionaire Asset Security System™, a key concern which absolutely must be addressed is how you plan to deal with the multitude of taxes, fees and other inhibitors to passing your wealth to your family and/or beneficiaries. By gaining a firm grasp on the myriad of issues surrounding the topic of estate planning, you can be rest assured that all that you have worked to accumulate during your lifetime will be put to your desired use after you've passed on.

What is estate planning?

The first question which absolutely must be answered in developing a good

understanding of the area of estate planning is, what is it? I firmly believe that most people have a bit of a misconception as to what estate planning is all about. For many people, estate planning means the process of drafting a will to determine who will receive your assets upon your death. While this is certainly part of it, there is a lot more to the process. It's not necessarily that simple.

Estate planning essentially refers to the area of analyzing an estate owner's financial affairs and developing a plan for how the owner's objectives can best be met. One definition of estate planning that I read in a book on the subject referred to it as "determining and expressing the method or methods of arranging or rearranging a person's property to accomplish the goals of the client." The book went on to state that the definition can be taken a bit further and be defined as "organizing the resources of the estate to adequately provide for the present and future needs of the surviving family." While I don't believe this to be the most complex definition I've ever seen of estate planning, it does little to shed any real light on the subject. It sounds nice and flowery, but it doesn't really answer our question. For our purposes, I want to give you a quick, simple definition of exactly what estate planning is all about.

Estate planning is about answering the questions of *who*, *what*, *where*, *when*, *why* and *how*. It's as simple as that. These are the questions that you need to answer in order to determine exactly what any subject is all about. Let's get into this in a bit more detail as it relates to the area of estate planning. In order to understand estate planning, the following questions must be answered:

- *Who* will receive the assets of your estate upon your death?

- ***What*** assets will you pass?
- ***Where*** can you go to get assistance in accomplishing your objectives?
- ***When*** should you pass your assets?
- ***Why*** do you need a formal estate plan?
- ***How*** can you best accomplish your objectives?

In a nutshell, this is as brief a definition as I can possibly give you. If you can get a handle on how you need to answer these questions, the estate planning process can be as simple and painless as possible. The rest of this chapter will be dedicated to helping you better understand the process of how you can answer these questions and hence, develop an effective estate plan.

To truly understand estate planning, you must understand why the process is so important. Estate planning is a process in which individuals attempt to maximum their wealth during their lifetime and pass the largest amount of assets possible to their loved ones at death with as little hassle as possible. This process, according to this definition, has three components:

1. Maximization of wealth
2. Minimizing estate and death taxes
3. Avoiding probate and will contests, if at all possible

The goal of estate planning is to pass as much as possible to your heirs, or whomever you wish (i.e. charity). The biggest obstacle to overcome in order to accomplish this goal is our beloved federal and state taxing authorities. Estate taxes can be as high as 55% to 60%. In case you are not that good at math, that is over half of your taxable estate.

Probate, which is discussed in more detail later in this book, is a legal night-mare most of us would like to avoid, but few of us can without proper plan-ning. The exorbitant legal costs coupled with the excessive time involved can and will make probate an individual's worst nightmare and an attorney's best friend.

In this book we will take a closer look at how to:

1. Maximize your wealth (business entities and retirement plans)
2. Minimize estate taxes (business entities and trusts)
3. Avoid probate and will contests (trusts)

Basically, estate planning is for everyone. To be blunt, we are all going to die. That means that estate planning will be a big part of our loved ones' future. The key is that now you have a say in what goes on. Tomorrow, you may not.

Why is estate planning important?

In deciding to set up a plan designed to combat any problem, it is crucial to understand the importance of overcoming that problem. We must come to understand the importance of estate planning by understanding the pitfalls which await us if we fail to implement an estate plan. It is perhaps most important to understand that estate planning is not just for the wealthy, but for anyone who owns assets.

Before we explore estate planning more fully, we will gain a wealth of under-standing about estate planning by learning why estate planning is so very vital, not just for the wealthy, but for everyone who wants to protect what they have

worked so hard to acquire.

We all like to believe that when we own property "free and clear" we are the sovereign owners of that property. After all, we worked hard to purchase, develop and maintain our properties. We follow the laws and pay our taxes, so therefore we have the *right* to pass on our possessions to whomever we choose and in whatever manner we choose, right? Not according to law. You own, make use of and transfer your property as a *privilege* not a right because of a concept known as "sovereign right." This concept states that a state has a right to property which precedes and supersedes the rights of individual citizens in order to provide for and protect the needs of the citizen body. Along with this goes the right to "eminent domain" or the right a state has to take, or more correctly to acquire, without consent but with compensation, a property needed for public purposes. This sovereign right gives the state the power to prescribe limitations, terms and conditions under which citizens may transfer property, even upon death. Five key conditions for transferring property include:

1.   The writing of a valid will. A will is a legal document by which an estate owner instructs the state on how he or she wishes the estate to be transferred. If there is no will, ownership of the property will be controlled by the state which will also determine how it will be distributed. Even small, modest estates should have the minimum of a valid will as an estate plan.

2.   A formal *administration of the estate*. In this condition, all the personal assets of the estate owner are collected, item-

ized and often valued for ultimate distribution. There are administration laws in each state which must be followed throughout this process. Depending on the size of the estate, the process may, in some cases, be under the control of the courts.

3. The payment of *debts* and *claims* for all obligations which were incurred while the owner of the estate lived. If there are not enough assets in the estate to cover all obligations, the states generally reserve the right to prioritize the claims against the estate.

4. The payment of state levied taxes. The state may require payment of a state estate tax, a state inheritance tax or sometimes both. An estate tax is a tax on the right to transfer the property at death and is based on the total value of the estate. An inheritance tax is a tax on the right of heirs to receive property transferred to them from a deceased estate owner and is based on the size of the share that each heir receives. Death taxes is a collective term for estate and inheritance taxes.

5. For estates exceeding the one-time federal credit and without proper estate planning strategies in place, a federal estate tax must be paid. This federal tax is imposed on the total value of the property transferred by the deceased.

This looks expensive!

As you may well have guessed by the simplified conditions above, this process can get expensive. Add to the taxes and fees above administrative expenses, funeral expenses, probate costs, accountant and attorney's fees and various state surcharges for filing and paperwork and the estate remaining for the heirs can be quickly reduced to half its original size. On top of this, if there is insufficient cash or other liquid assets on hand to pay these costs, other

Without proper planning, these costs can substantially reduce the estate that you leave for your heirs.

assets will have to be liquidated in order to pay them. Without proper planning, these costs can substantially reduce the estate that you leave for your heirs. Why work your whole life in order to provide for your family after your death, only to leave your loved ones burdened with debts and loss due to improper or inadequate planning? By employing the strategies of the Secret Millionaire, you can alleviate a great deal of this problem.

Too often, we follow the misconception that when we die, our estate will simply be "signed over" to our heirs just the way we left it for them, or that my estate isn't large or valuable enough to be taxed or go through probate courts. These can be very expensive and time-consuming misconceptions for our loved ones. These misconceptions are usually results of:

- lack of experience with estate probate, the probate process and estate administration.

- the belief that what we leave for our heirs will be treated for taxation as "gifts" during our lifetime, though there is a large difference between the two.

- the erroneous belief that estate costs and taxes are applicable only to the wealthy and therefore, only the wealthy need estate planning.

The unfortunate truth is that many of us have these misconceptions and fail to plan our estates properly if we make any plans at all. If you fail to implement a proper estate plan, your heirs may be faced with paying the maximum in taxes, fees and other costs for your estate. They may have to pay for what you may regard as "rightfully theirs."

What is involved in the overall estate planning process?

The first step in estate planning is the same as the first step in virtually any well thought out plan, define the goals and objectives that you want the plan to achieve. If you don't decide in the beginning where you are going, you cannot efficiently choose how and when to get there. Think about this as a journey. You must first decide where you are going and when you want to go before you ever begin packing your suitcase of car. Otherwise you can end up with shorts and swimwear for a trip to Iceland, or booking boat passage for a hiking trip.

> *If you don't decide in the beginning where you are going, you cannot choose how and when to get there.*

Before you ever go see a professional, decide what you want to do with your estate, then the professional can more quickly and efficiently design a plan that will help you get there. "But they are the professionals," you say. That's exactly right, but do you want to pay these professionals as much as $450 or $500 per hour to help you decide to whom you want to give your estate when you die? That's for you to do. Their job is then made much easier and more

efficient. You see, when you tell them where you want to go, they have a whole arsenal of estate planning tools to help you get there. Then they can simply design a plan using these tools to help you reach *your* goals.

Also, failure to define your goals and objectives can get expensive in other ways as well. If you change your mind frequently, do you think your financial professional is going to change your whole estate plan, tax filings, legal fees and hourly wages included, for free? Of course not! You will be charged for your changes to your estate plan. And remember that this is a *plan*. It has many parts which function in different ways to achieve your ultimate estate planning goals. When you change one part of the plan, you may have to change others. Ouch! This can begin to add up quickly.

Changing your estate plan is not always a bad thing, it may be necessary and beneficial after changes in your situation. You should review your estate plan periodically with your estate planning professional to make certain that your plan is still current. Changes such as the birth or death of a beneficiary, property or asset purchase or sale, or changes in marital status may necessitate changes in your estate plan. If you have had the same estate plan for forty years, your family may be in for as much grief as one without any plan at all.

I see people daily who are concerned with implementing legal entities to help them build and protect their assets and estates during their lives. We all want the "American dream" and can spend our lives working to achieve it. I also see these same people who work so diligently to protect their assets today risk losing as much as half their estate to the expenses mentioned earlier. This is not exactly what they had in mind as a way to transfer the fruits of their life's work.

This situation can sneak up on you far too easily. Take life insurance policies, for example. Many, many people have multiple life insurance policies purchased at different times in their lives and from various agents. Most people don't realize, because they have not been told, that they should have a coordinated plan that encompasses all of their insurance policies and the distribution of the benefits of these policies. Most people also don't realize, again from not being informed, that the benefits of most of these insurance policies are included in the total value of their taxable estate upon their death. Even if you have written a will, your will may not be current with your new, additional insurance policies or beneficiary changes on current insurance policies. The will or benefit disbursement may also not allow for payment of these benefits in a manner which will let the heirs use the proceeds to cover their tax and fee burden.

Take a look at the following example and see if your estate planning, or lack thereof is in better or worse condition:

Jon Louis worked very hard his entire life to provide for his family and to build his construction business so that they would have a means of income when he was gone. At his death, his business was worth more than one million dollars, he owned a four-unit apartment building from which he collected rent, made repairs, paid taxes, etc., and he owned some undeveloped property in an area which he had hoped would boom and earn a tidy profit for him or his family. But Jon had no comprehensive estate plan in place.

In his life insurance policy, Jon's widow, Marie, would receive a single sum payout of $10,000 with the rest of the proceeds to be paid to her as life income.

Jon had left a will, which stated that the business and vacant property were to be left in a trust with the annual income from the business to be paid to Marie until her death, at which time the income would go to their daughter, Jackie. Jon had given Jackie the apartment building as a gift the year before his death, but he had remained in control of the building, thus a tax court ruled that it was not truly gifted away and included the building in Jon's taxable estate.

Because Jon's widow, Marie was left with a lack of cash or other liquid assets to pay funeral, administrative and estate tax costs, Marie had to sell the business and the undeveloped property at a loss to meet expenses. Marie properly gifted the remaining apartment building to her daughter, Jackie, and was left with only the proceeds from Jon's life insurance policy as income.

Jon had attempted to provide for his family by gifting the apartment to his daughter, though not properly, providing for his wife with a life income from his life insurance, though he did not realize the need for cash to pay funeral and estate tax expenses, and a will which was not coordinated with his other measures. A well coordinated and properly implemented estate plan could have avoided all of these estate planning problems.

As mentioned earlier, defining your goals and objectives should be done before you begin the actual estate planning process. I mention this again only because it is so important. Once you have defined these goals and objectives, a detailed design or blueprint of your financial position should be drawn up. There are five successive steps that are crucial to creating and maintaining your estate plan. These are what we refer to as the five steps in the Secret Millionaire estate planning process:

1. **Documentation**—You and your financial professional should assemble all the pertinent facts about your material resources and assets and the personal and financial circumstances of each member of the family or potential heirs. In doing this, you should take into account both past and potential behavior, family changes (marriage, births, divorce, deaths, etc.), financial status and responsibility, etc.

2. **Analysis**—Analyze these facts and compare them against your goals and objectives.

3. **Formulation**—Formulate potential plans, then test them and select the one which most helps you to reach your estate planning goals.

4. **Implementation**—Implement your estate plan. No plan can be successful unless it is implemented.

5. **Review and Revision**—Perform periodic reviews and revise the estate plan.

Let's look at each of these steps in more detail.

Step 1: Documentation

Your estate planning professional will need what amounts to a financial inventory of your and your family's assets. This inventory will start with a "roll call" of each member of your family. Their age, relationship, education, overall

health and occupation will be included in this fact finding stage. Any property owned by each person will be included in this inventory as well as any current plan for distribution of assets, such as wills, trusts, insurance policies, retirement plans, etc. One great way to do this is to get a copy of the book *MillionHeirs*. It is the best book available for providing blueprints for your beneficiaries. To order, call Profit Publishing Group, Inc. toll-free at 877.868.9742. Remember also that in this phase, your goals and objectives for your estate plan should be made clear to your estate planning professional.

Step 2: Analysis

In this step, any weaknesses in your current situation should be located and corrected, and any strengths should be reinforced. Your financial planner should put your estate through a simulated probate to reveal into which of three transfer methods your property will fall. This exercise will determine whether your assets will pass:

1.   to your estate;

2.   outside the probate estate by reason of law (i.e. joint ownership); or

3.   outside the probate estate under terms of a legal contract (i.e. death benefits or life insurance).

If the property passes to the estate, your estate planner will further classify the assets into assets that:

1.   represent liquid assets (cash or its equivalent);

2.   can be converted into cash; and

3.   will be distributed to the estate's beneficiaries.

If the estate owner is married, the property should further be classified into assets that:

1.   qualify for the unlimited marital deduction; or

2.   do not qualify for this deduction.

An estimate must be made of all asset and property values, as well as debts, claims and expenses of estate administration. These estimates are necessary in order to calculate current estate death taxes.

If the estate owner is married, calculations will have to be made for two situations, one in which the estate owner dies first and then the spouse dies, or in which the spouse dies first and then the estate owner. Both of these calculations are very important as the estate death taxes may be very different for the two situations.

By calculating multiple scenarios, the professional is able to more accurately calculate the amount of cash needed to pay debts, taxes, estate administrative costs, and to provide cash to your beneficiaries to provide for daily necessities and expenses. This will also bring to light any unexpected expenses or problems which might arise. Think back to our Jon Louis example and how

the apartment building that he gifted to his daughter to provide for her turned into a cash drain because he had not planned properly.

With this analysis, you can further examine the suitability of estate assets and learn whether or not these assets will provide adequate income for your survivors. An analysis of Jon Louis's situation would have revealed that his business, though worth over a million dollars while alive, became a severe liability to the estate when he died. Had this analysis been performed, the problem could have been corrected before it cost his widow her main means of income. Problems like inadequate funds for funeral costs, incapacitated or unskilled heirs who need the income from a business, but who are unable to operate the business properly, or even outright transfer of property to minor children, which can result in expensive guardianships can be revealed and solutions implemented.

If your estate plan was drafted prior to the 1981 unlimited marital deduction or the repeal in 1990 of the Internal Revenue Code (IRC) estate freeze provisions, your will or plan may no longer be appropriate for your estate and may actually contradict your current needs and objectives.

Step 3: Formulation

All possible arrangements that can logically fulfill your goals and objectives should be considered in this step. By doing so, the best solution for each problem or situation found in the previous step can be determined.

Using the three estate transfer methods mentioned earlier, namely: (1) assets transferred to the estate; (2) assets that will pass outside of the probate

estate by law; and, (3) assets that will pass outside of the estate according to the terms of a contract; the current plan and possible arrangements can be formulated and tested. Perhaps placing your property or assets into a trust might be a better solution than passing it by means of a will. In Jon Louis's example, if he had gifted the apartment to his daughter outright during his lifetime, it would not have been part of his taxable estate.

By doing this testing and analysis process, problems and solutions can be worked out before the situation presents itself and a blueprint developed of your estate plan. You can then have a clear picture of the manner in which your survivors will be provided for after your death.

Step 4: Implementation

> *The first mistake people make is by not having a plan, the second mistake is in not implementing a plan.*

In this step you must put into action the developments and entities that were determined to be the best for your situation in Step 3. You may have to purchase additional life insurance or have your attorney prepare new wills, trusts, deeds or contracts in order to put your plan into action. The first mistake people make is by not having a plan, the second mistake is in not implementing a plan. Having a plan and not putting it into action is just as devastating as having no plan at all.

Step 5: Review and Revision

Changes in your familial or financial situation inevitably occur. So do changes in the tax code and in law. It is therefore necessary to make periodic reviews

of your estate plan so that needed changes or revisions can be made with the least amount of headache. How often you do this is, of course, based on your particular situation. If your tax attorney or accountant is a member of your estate planning team, then discussing your estate plan at tax preparation time can be a good rule of thumb. You are already there and paying for your professional's time, so a quick glance over your plan will not take up much time or money for either of you.

The estate planning team brings me to another point, one which I repeat over and over because I feel it is vitally important to your financial planning, the *Master Mind Team*.

Your team always includes yourself, a tax attorney, and your tax accountant and for estate planning may include a trust professional. Your team members must function as one in planning for your financial well being. You, as the person with the most to lose and gain must keep your team members informed about each other and your goals and objectives. In a properly structured *Master Mind Team,* each member can contribute his or her particular skills, expertise and experience to the five steps of the estate planning process.

What tools are available for estate planning?

There are several basic tools which can be called the fundamental tools or strategies for any estate plan. These basic tools include:

- a will
- trusts
- the estate marital deduction

- gift tax strategies
- lifetime gifts
- life insurance, as used strategically in the overall plan

A more in depth look at each of these tools will reveal their uses in the estate planning process.

Wills

Though there are many methods and strategies for formulating an effective estate plan, the best known and most often used (often inefficiently) is the will. Wills, or in some cases, living trusts, are the foundation or the cornerstone of the successful estate plan.

Through your will or living trust, you can direct the disposition of your property after your death. The primary function of both of these documents is the same, to transfer the estate owner's assets to surviving heirs in the manner in which the estate owner outlined. They can also contain provisions which will allow the estate owner to complete certain actions which were begun while the estate owner lived, such as transfer ownership or management of a business or a final gift to a charity.

If you die with a will, you are said to have died *testate*. Those who die without a will or with an invalid will are said to have died *intestate*. If the estate owner dies *intestate* it is the state's right and duty to essentially create one for him or her under the state's corresponding intestacy laws. These laws pass property based on family relationships and are expensive and inefficient. In order to minimize estate costs or estate shrinkage, effective estate planning

requires a minimum of a valid will.

Remember that your will is revocable and changeable during life and does not come into effect until death. A will also ONLY affects the situation that occurs on the date of death, any property which is outside the scope of the will must still be probated.

Trusts

A trust is a legal contract in which property is given by the grantor to another individual or corporate entity called a trustee, for the benefit of a third party or beneficiary. The trustee is granted the deed or ownership to the property or assets and charged with handling the assets according to the wishes of the grantor. These wishes are outlined in the contract or trust agreement and the trustee must abide by these terms. Trusts, through the proper structuring and use of powers over trust assets, enable grantors to provide beneficiaries with most of the benefits of property ownership. Depending on the specific purpose and structure of the trust, there may be tax advantages associated with placing assets into a trust. For more information on trusts, see the chapter devoted to that topic in this book.

Estate tax marital deduction

The unlimited federal estate tax marital deduction can present an important advantage for an estate owner married to a spouse who owns little property. Under this deduction, much of the tax which would otherwise by payable upon the death of the first spouse to pass can be postponed by passing the property to the surviving spouse. Since only certain property qualifies for the

marital deduction, proper planning must be done in order to take full advantage of the benefits. Your estate planning professional will usually begin by the qualification of property that passes outside the probate estate, such as life insurance proceeds payable to the spouse, as well as property passing under the terms and provisions of your will. The unlimited marital deduction may provide no benefits when the second spouse passes if both couples own equal or approximately equal amounts of property.

Even with this deduction, a coordinated estate plan is necessary to protect the estate from a significant tax burden on the passing of the second spouse, especially in situations in which the estate experiences rapid growth after the death of the first spouse. A good estate plan will include strategies and provisions to minimize that tax burden.

Gift tax privileges

A person is allowed to "gift away" up to $10,000 in cash or property per person to any number of donees each year without having to pay the federal gift tax. If that person has a spouse, he or she also has the same gifting privilege. This means that a couple with five children could gift away as much as $20,000 to each child, each year. That comes to $100,000 per year gifted away free of federal gift taxes. This can be very effective in reducing estate taxes as most of the gifts will not be included in the donor's estate at death. This measure can be extremely effective when used in a situation such as the one mentioned above, where assets experience rapid growth after the death of the first spouse. Removing those assets from the surviving spouse's estate can significantly reduce the estate's tax burden.

Lifetime gifts

A lifetime gift is a gift of property or assets given away during the donor's life. The strategy behind this is that if the property is given away during life, it will not be included in the donor's estate at death. There may also be annual income tax savings for the donor as well as reductions in estate costs and administrative expenses. In order to qualify for lifetime gift status, however, the donor must relinquish all control over the assets and give up all rights to the income from the property or assets. The donor must, therefore, make certain that the recipients are mature and experienced enough to handle the property or assets properly.

Life insurance

The true value of the life insurance policy becomes glaringly evident in the area of estate planning. Life insurance policies can be essential in providing cash for funeral expenses, federal estate taxes and state death taxes, and administrative costs. In our Jon Louis example, his life insurance policy did not provide his widow with enough cash to cover these costs and her estate assets had to be sold at "forced sale" prices in order to raise the needed cash. When insurance proceeds are passed outside the estate, the proceeds are received tax-free by the beneficiary. Though proceeds are included in the taxable estate when they are paid directly to the personal representative of the estate, much needed cash to meet estate settlement costs can be a much more important benefit. The more quickly the estate settlement costs can be met, the more quickly the net estate can be distributed to the heirs.

Life insurance can also play a major role in providing necessary funding for

business continuation plans, trusts, charitable contributions, and income for beneficiaries.

When is the best time to begin your estate plan?

Unfortunately, proper estate planning is one of the most overlooked areas of overall financial planning. This is mainly because people just simply do not like to think about their eventual death. Let's face it, this is not a very fun subject. However, once you have passed away, you really don't have much say in what goes on with your property. You definitely have lost your ability to defend yourself against the IRS. The fact is, the

> *...once you have passed away, you really don't have much to say in what goes on with your property.*

best time to begin your estate planning strategy is today, while you are still alive. We know we are not guaranteed much else.

Right now you can still determine whether or not you need a living trust to avoid probate. You can implement a gifting strategy, which can save eventual estate taxes. You can decide to pass business interests on to heirs. You can structure the ownership and beneficiaries of your life insurance policies to help taxes. The reality is, right now you get to make the decision. Once you are gone, those decisions will be made by someone else who may not have the same goals as you.

The other thing I need to point out is that estate planning is for everyone, even for those who do not have large enough estates to pay estate and death taxes. Most estates will go through probate. This is a very painful and expensive process discussed later in this book.

Last year a friend of mine lost his father in an automobile accident. His dad was forty-six. My friend came from a middle-class family that never thought probate and estate taxes would be in their future, much less their immediate future. The accident was caused by another driver, therefore, the insurance payoffs were quite significant. My friend's family had to wade through the nightmare of probate before they could settle the simplest of insurance claims. All of this cost them attorney's fees, interest on the proceeds, not to mention the anxiety of dealing with this mess immediately after this tragedy. The sad thing is, my friend was a CPA. The thought of a living trust for his family had never entered his mind, even though he had advised many clients to do so on a routine basis.

My point from this story is this: Estate planning is for everyone. Just because you may not be monetarily rich does not mean that this is an area that you personally do not need to address. Your actions today can and will save your family untold grief and anxiety in the future.

How can I learn more about and establish an estate plan?

I see everyday how confusing the legal and accounting aspect of estate planning can be. One of the reasons I went into the legal field was to learn for myself what all the jargon meant so that I could help myself and my family in our personal and financial lives. I quickly realized that the majority of people out there were just like my family, so I dedicated myself to making the information available to everyone in a simple, understandable format. The sage humorist and critic Will Rogers remarked in 1927 that, "the minute you read something and can't understand it, you can almost be sure that it was drawn

> *"The minute you read something and can't understand it, you can almost be sure that it was drawn up by a lawyer."* -Will Rogers

up by a lawyer." This statement is sadly as true today as it was nearly 72 years ago. There are only a few good sources of information available for the average individual. I have dedicated my practice and my company to providing quality material with clear illustrations and explanations so that the basic concepts become evident.

The area of estate planning is one of crucial significance to becoming a Secret Millionaire. Learning about the inner workings of estate planning and the tools involved in the overall process is an absolute must. It is such an integral part of the overall process that you simply cannot leave yourself without the knowledge of how the various legal entities can and do work for providing estate planning and helping you to accomplish key wealth objectives. Profit Publishing Group, Inc. has developed books, audio and video tapes, software, and educational seminars designed to help you gain the necessary understanding of this important area. Not only that, they also help individuals establish the most effective estate plans possible. If you are ready to take control of your finances and provide for your heirs and beneficiaries, call toll-free at 877.868.9742. Call today!

"Difficulties mastered are opportunities won."
Churchill

Chapter IV
Secret Millionaire
Tax Planning

O ne of the key distinctions between the Secret Millionaire and others is the way in which they perceive the world around them. It has been said that every difficult situation poses an opportunity for those who are ready to recognize it and overcome the adversity. Secret Millionaires pride themselves on being able to see opportunity where others see only problems. That is the key to

> *Secret Millionaires pride themselves on being able to see opportunity where others see only problems.*

their success. In this chapter, you will discover an area that can pose tremendous opportunities where most see nothing more than difficulties.

When dealing with difficult situations, perhaps none is more trying than the United States Tax Code. Our tax code is made up of literally thousands of pages of rules, regulations, and laws which must be abided by in order to avoid serious trouble with the agency that governs compliance of those laws, the Internal Revenue Service (IRS). In the Service's defense, I will say that they try to make things as simple as possible. However, as often happens, trying to simplify something often tends to make it much more difficult. When it comes to the Internal Revenue Code, this is certainly the case.

Let me give you a brief example of what I am talking about. The tax code is made up of numerous sections which govern how you pay your taxes in vari-

ous situations. The IRS has tried to make things as simple as possible in this code. As such, they have even included a "definitions" section of the code to explain any terms that may be difficult to understand. As an attorney, I deal with numerous statutes and codes all the time and one of the key concepts to understand is that a word is to be read as the enactor of the statute intended it. The best way to understand how the enactor meant the word to be read is to look it up in the "definitions" section. Let's give it a shot.

Let's presume for the moment that I am interested in looking up the definition of "husband and wife". Now wait a second. You may be saying to yourself, "Why would I have to look up the definition for 'husband and wife'? Everyone knows what 'husband and wife' are, even those who aren't even married." The problem with your rationale is that you are applying common sense. There is no room for common sense when it comes to interpreting the tax code.

We now turn in our trusty tax code to the "definitions" section and look up our term. Here is the definition straight from the code:

Section 7701. Definitions

STATUTE

(a)   When used in this title, where not otherwise distinctly expressed or manifestly incompatible with the intent thereof-

   (17) Husband and Wife

As used in sections 152 (b)(4), 682, and 2516, if the husband and wife therein referred to are divorced, wherever appropriate to the meaning of such sections, the term 'wife' shall be read 'former wife' and the term husband shall be read 'former husband'; and, if the payments described in such sections are made by or on behalf of the wife or former wife to the husband or former husband instead of vice versa, wherever appropriate to the meaning of such sections, the term 'husband' shall be read 'wife' and the term 'wife' shall be read 'husband'.

Does that clear things up for you? After reading that definition, many people aren't quite sure which one they are. I think that perhaps the scariest thing is that I believe that I actually do understand it.

I gave you this example to illustrate a couple of points. The first point you need to understand is that the tax code is extremely difficult to truly comprehend. For this reason, most people decide that it's easiest to just give up and simply fork over whatever they think they have to pay, regardless of whether they could have reduced this amount. The second point is that I want to underscore the importance of knowledge. If the tax code is this complex and difficult to comprehend, it seems elementary that you would need to hire an experienced guide who has the knowledge and know-how to direct you through the proverbial jungle which is the tax code. The problem is that most people try to make it without that much-needed guide or to not even give it a shot at all.

A good tax practitioner, by that I mean a good tax accountant or tax attorney, is worth their weight in gold if they can help you effectively manage your tax

obligation. For that reason, I have associated my good friend and top-notch tax accountant, Johnny Tollett, to assist clients with their specific tax matters. He has not only a wealth of knowledge and real world experience, but also a real talent for taking complex tax issues and putting them into language that anyone can understand. As such, he has assisted immensely with this book and especially with this chapter by illustrating important aspects of legal entities through the use of examples to help you better learn the material.

In preparing literally thousands of tax returns, he has experienced just about every type of question that might potentially pop up. In this chapter, he lays out the mechanics of tax planning with some great examples to illustrate those key points. The straight-forward nature of it will help you to gain a better grasp on the underlying principles which make up our tax system. Once you learn these principles, you will be better situated to handle your tax situation.

There are certainly ways to reduce your taxes. Unfortunately, the only way to do that is to learn what you're up against. As the quote at the beginning of this chapter states, "Difficulties mastered are opportunities won." Making the most out of every tax break you are entitled to can mean a huge difference in how you view the tax code and how you conduct your life and business. Let's get started by providing an answer to the primary question on an often misunderstood topic, what exactly is tax planning?

What is tax planning?

Tax planning is a process by which an individual sets up his or her financial situation in a way that legally allows them to pay the least amount of tax allowed under the tax laws. Now let me ask you, do you agree or disagree with

this practice? I have yet to give one seminar or have one consultation where anyone answered "no" to this question. The simple fact is we all want to pay the government less and keep more of our hard-earned money. Why is it then, when I ask people what tax saving strategies they have implemented for themselves, they have no answer?

I believe the answer to this question actually is part of the definition of tax planning given above. First, tax planning is for individuals, all individuals. Most hard-working taxpayers believe that tax planning is only for the wealthy. While this small segment of society definitely utilizes tax strategies to their financial benefit, tax planning is by no means limited to individuals with six figure plus incomes. Secondly, tax planning is one hundred percent legal. People around the country have constantly asked me if the techniques I use to reduce taxes are legal. Perhaps the best way to illustrate the legality of reducing one's taxes is to take a look at one of my favorite quotes by one of my favorite judges, Judge Learned Hand:

> *"There is nothing sinister in arranging one's affairs as to keep taxes as low as possible...for nobody owes any public duty to pay more than the law demands."*
> **Judge Learned Hand**

Remember, the IRS Tax Code is a matter of law. This law just happens to be the most difficult and complex set of laws our country has to offer. If these techniques work for the big boys, they can work for you. The key is to learn what those laws are and how they can be used for your particular situation.

The focus of this chapter is to explain in simple, straight-forward terms exactly what tax planning is and how it can work for you. I believe a big stumbling block when it comes to tax planning comes from the tax preparers and CPAs we come in contact with. They simply cannot relay to you, the taxpayer, in concise, easily understood terms what you specifically have to do to reduce your tax bill. A couple of years ago, my brother-in-law finally called to ask for some financial advice. When we got to the subject of taxes, I asked him what his CPA had suggested he do. After a one and a half hour consultation with his trusted CPA, all my brother-in-law could remember was, "have some kids and buy a house." While these two tax planning "strategies" can definitely reduce taxes, they are not something you can implement on a year-by-year basis. This source of advice cost my brother-in-law $175.

The most important thing for you to understand is that tax planning is 100% legal and is available for anyone who will take the time to learn how to do it. The biggest problem is that people fail to realize that they indeed have a choice as to whether or not they want to reduce their tax bills. The key is to take things seriously and understand the importance of planning your tax situation rather than simply taking what's given to you.

Why is tax planning so important?

Have you ever heard the term "default judgment"? Do you know what it means? It is a legal term for a situation in which a party does not defend itself before the court and, therefore, takes the judgment levied by the court based only on the suing party's view of the dispute. In the legal context, this means that if you fail to defend yourself, you automatically lose. It is as if you are agreeing to the other party's accusations whether you believe them to be cor-

rect or not. Now I don't know about you, but if I get sued, and I know I am right, you better believe I will defend myself. Wouldn't you? Of course you would.

The sad thing about this legal situation is that it happens to practically every taxpaying American every year. Let's insert characters to this legal situation. You, the taxpayer, are the one being sued. The IRS is suing you. Even though there are means out there to reduce your tax bill, you do nothing and pay the IRS the amount they say you owe.

Think about this for a little while. Am I over exaggerating the situation or is this really what happens? If this doesn't make you at least take the initiative to implement some form of tax saving strategies, you can continue to add yourself to the long list of taxpayers who pay more than they probably should.

Let's put this into dollar amounts. Assume you are in the 28% income tax bracket. Under current law, that's about $30,000 a year for single taxpayers and $55,000 a year for married taxpayers. If you can implement techniques and strategies to reduce your taxable income by $3000, that results in a tax savings to you of $840. This does not count the amount of state income taxes you would save. If it works in one year, it will probably work in following years in which you might be in a higher tax bracket. This could add up to a substantial amount of money, and that is with only reducing your taxable income by $3000, a mere 10%. Is this possible? Easily. The great part is when you start finding a lot of these strategies which can be easily implemented to your situation.

One of the primary reasons that people pay too much in taxes is that they do

not fully understand how income is taxed. For most, they think that all income is taxed the same way and at the same rates which keeps them from maximizing their tax savings. A simple understanding of the different types of income taxes can mean a great deal of money to you each and every year in the form of tax savings. With that thought in mind, let's discuss the different types.

What are the different types of income taxes?

As we pointed out, a big problem with taxpayers today is that they simply do not know just exactly how they are taxed. And for good reason, even the most educated of tax professionals have to refer to resources to determine how certain items will be taxed. Below is a list of the most common types of income taxes. Notice, we are not dealing with state issues in this section. Those taxes are in addition to the bill you pile up with the Feds. Let's take a look.

1. Income Taxes

This is the most basic of all taxes. Income taxes are progressive. This means the more you make, the larger percentage you pay. In essence, you are penalized for making more money. We won't go there for now. Below are the Federal Income Tax Tables for single and married individuals for the 1998 tax year.

Single		Married	
$ 0- $25,350	15%	$ 0- $42,350	15%
$ 25,351- $61,400	28%	$ 42,351- $102,300	28%

$ 61,401- $128,100	31%	$ 102,301- $155,950	31%
$ 128,101- $278,450	36%	$ 155,951- $278,450	36%
$ 278,451 & Over	39.6%	$ 278,451 & Over	39.6%

The dollar values listed above represent taxable income amounts, not gross income amounts. Taxable income is gross income minus the standard deduction **or** itemized deductions (but not both) and minus personal exemptions.

One of the most common mistakes people make when looking at a table like this is to remember that income taxes are progressive. If your taxable income is $40,000 and you are single, you owe 15% on the first $25,350 and 28% on the excess. You do not owe 28% on the entire amount. While this may seem basic to some of you reading this, it's surprising to see how many people fail to understand this concept.

Income taxes are what you get refunds from, if you are so lucky, come tax time. They are automatically withheld from your paycheck at a rate based on the information you put on form W-4 when you began your employment with your present company. Your current amount paid in should be identifiable on your pay stub by "Federal Income Taxes Withheld", or "FWH", or something similar. Self-employed individuals pay in income taxes by making estimated tax payments throughout the year

As you can see, the biggest tax jump comes at the 15-28% border. Your tax basically doubles once you graduate into a 28% bracket. It is when income begins to slide into this range that I see taxpayers, usually married taxpayers, scrambling to come up with money to pay Uncle Sam on April 15th. The bad news is it only gets worse as you improve yourself financially. One of the most

basic steps in tax planning is to determine what tax bracket you are in. A key tax strategy is to do whatever it takes to lower this bracket. We will be discussing ways to do that later in this chapter.

2. Social Security and Medicare Taxes (FICA)

No other tax seems to bother people more than this one, especially self-employed individuals. Social security taxes are paid at a rate of 6.2%. This is 6.2% for both the employee and the employer. Thus, a self-employed individual is paying at a rate of 12.4%. For employees, social security is automatically deducted from your paycheck. You will feel better knowing that none of this tax is refunded come tax time. It will most definitely be put aside by our federal government to help provide for you and your family during your retirement years. It is important to note that social security taxes stop once an employee has taxable income of $72,600 (for tax year 1999).

Medicare is another part of FICA that helps ensure our golden years. It is paid at a rate of 1.45% for employees and employers (2.9% for self-employed individuals). None of this tax is refundable, either. Unlike social security taxes, there is no dollar limit where Medicare taxes phase out.

Simple math can show you that FICA taxes come to 7.65% for employees and 15.3% for self-employed individuals. FICA taxes are paid on earned income. The most common form of earned income is W-2 wages. Earned income also comes from net income from a sole-proprietorship and income from partnerships.

If we look at it this way, the least amount of tax a self-employed individual

could pay is 30.3% (15% income tax and 15.3% FICA tax). If you fall into this category, chances are you are not overly happy with your current tax situation. Do you think you like the idea of a default tax judgment now?

3. Capital Gains Taxes

Before we get too excited about capital gain rates, let's clarify short term and long term capital gains. A couple of years ago, this section would take up a whole chapter, if not the whole book. Thanks to some measure of tax simplification, short term capital gains apply to investments held one year or less. Long term capital gains apply to investments held more than one year.

Taxes on short term gains are taxed at the same rates as listed earlier under the income tax section. However, the good news is that short term capital gains are not subject to FICA taxes. This makes this type of income more preferable than ordinary earned income.

Long term capital gains are given preferential treatment under the code. They are taxed at 20% (10% if you fall in the 15% income tax bracket). They are also exempt from FICA taxes thus making them more preferable than both ordinary earned income as well as short term capital gains.

A good solid understanding of these three types of taxes goes a long way in forming an effective tax planning strategy.

Types of income

All right, it's time for a pop quiz. Below, I have listed some different types of

income. What I want you to do is rank these in the order you would like to receive them. Try not to look ahead at the way I have answered them, let's just see how we compare at this point. We have discussed some of the items, some we have not. Here's the list.

Short term capital gain   _____
Interest and Dividends   _____
Tax free income   _____
Earned income   _____
Long term capital gain   _____
Rents and Royalties   _____
Deferred Income   _____

The list above represents essentially all of the different categories of income and how income may be characterized. What I want you to do is list these types of income in the order you would like to receive them from a taxation point of view.

What factors did you use in ranking these types of income? If you can answer this question on these different categories, you are well on your way to understanding how tax planning can and will benefit you. Now, list what percentage of your personal income comes from each of these categories. How close are you to where you would like to be from a taxation standpoint? Don't get too worried if you are far from this. The nature of your income may be difficult to change. Our goal is to help you to effectively manage your current situation.

Let's look at how I ranked each of the categories of income. I have also given this pop quiz to some colleagues of mine and their answers mirrored the ones

I have come up with.

1. Tax free income: Income with no tax is better than the alternative.

2. Deferred income: This is the same thing as an interest free loan. It's difficult to pass up free money.

3. Long term capital gains: LTCG are taxed at lower rates and are not subject to FICA taxes. They are also not taxed until the investment is sold.

4. Rents and Royalties: These are taxed at regular income tax rates and not subject to FICA. However, expenses can be deducted from these to reach the taxable amount.

5. Short term capital gains: STCG are taxes at ordinary income rates and are not subject to FICA. They are more attractive than interest and dividends because the option is there to hold them for a long term period.

6. Interest and Dividends: These are taxed at regular income tax rates and not subject to FICA.

7. Earned Income: Taxed at regular income tax rates and subject to FICA.

The order is obviously dictated by lowest tax rates, avoidability of FICA, and the ability to deduct expenses to reduce taxable income. Now, look at the

percentages of each of these that make up your financial portfolio. Something tells me that 95-100% of your personal income comes from the earned (W-2) income category. Why is it that the obvious last choice of type of income is overwhelmingly the type we all have? Remember the concept of default tax judgment? We do not attempt to change our tax status, therefore, the IRS levies the worst of all taxes on us.

Now let me ask you, if I could show you ways to legally transfer some earned income into these other categories, would you be interested? If you answered "no", all you have to do is close this book and continue paying the default tax judgment that the IRS imposes on you. If you answered "yes", the rest of this book could prove to be invaluable not only to you, but to your family as well.

Tax Planning Techniques Anyone Can Use

A very common statement I hear from clients and from those attending my seminars is, "My wife and I only make $70,000 a year, we have one child and a mortgage. After paying for childcare and all of our living expenses we just don't have the money to start tax planning. We live from paycheck to paycheck." This situation may describe many of you reading this book. An important point for you to understand is that virtually anyone can

An important point for you to understand is that virtually anyone can obtain some tax relief through proper tax planning.

obtain some tax relief through proper tax planning. To see a few simple ways, let's put some numbers to this situation and see if we can help.

	Taxpayer	Spouse
Name	Jack	Jane
Occupation	Computer Programmer	Dental Assistant
Salary	$40,000	$30,000

Jack and Jane have one son Joe, age 10. Jack and Jane itemize their deductions with the following expenses:

Mortgage Interest:	$5000
Taxes	$3000
Church Contributions	$2000

Additional information is as follows:

Child care costs:	$100 per week
Credit Card Debt:	$4000 @ 18% $100 monthly payment
Auto Loan	$10,000 @ 10% $350 monthly payment
Student Loans	$8000 @ 8% $250 monthly payment
Mortgage	$70,000 @ 7% $800 monthly payment
Market Value of Home $100,000	
Original Price of Home $90,000	

Jack and Jane are contemplating having another child, but are concerned about the monthly expenses that come with children. They are comfortable with their home and are not planning on moving in the near future.

I have a feeling that this scenario is not that uncommon among taxpayers today. Let's look at their situation. Jack and Jane's current tax liability can be computed as follows.

Gross Income	$70,000
Itemized Deductions	($10,000)
Personal Exemptions	($8100)
Taxable Income	$51,900
Income Tax	$9034
Child Care Credit	($480)
Net Taxes for Year	$8554

Let's remember this scenario. Jack and Jane's tax liability is $8554 with monthly debt service of $1500.

Tax Planning Technique #1

Jack and Jane pay childcare expenses of $5200 per year. They received a credit for childcare costs of $480 dollars on their tax return. What would happen if Jack elects to be covered under his employer's dependent care benefit plan? If he does, Jack can elect to exclude as much as $5000 from his taxable income. From our income tax lesson earlier, we know that Jack and Jane are in the 28% tax bracket. Five thousand dollars in a 28% bracket results in a tax savings of $1400. Remember also in our tax discussion that earned income is subject to FICA. The employees share of FICA is 7.65%, or another $383 in tax savings. The combination of these two events gives them a tax savings of $1783. Compared to the $480 credit they would have received if they accepted the IRS default judgment, electing this type of tax

treatment just put $1303 in their bank account.

Tax Planning Technique #2

Jack and Jane have been married for 15 years and have accumulated quite a few household goods over time. It would be no problem at all for them to give $500 worth of goods a year to charities such as the Salvation Army or Goodwill. This $500 donation is an itemized deduction in the 28% tax bracket. Thus, another tax savings of $140.

Tax Planning Technique #3

Jack and Jane currently have two types of interest, mortgage interest and personal interest. Mortgage interest is deductible as an itemized deduction. Personal interest is not deductible at all. They have personal debt of $22,000 (Credit cards, auto loan, and student loans). They have plenty of equity in their home ($30,000) and can get the same interest rate they currently have. Raising their mortgage to $92,000 would increase their mortgage interest to $7500 per year. This is $2500 more than it was before. In a 28% tax bracket, this is a tax savings of $700. What's more, their monthly payment only went up $50 per month. By converting personal debt to mortgage debt, Jack and Jane's monthly personal debt service which was $700 per month has now been reduced to nothing. With an increase on their mortgage of only $50, they now have added $650 to their monthly cash flow.

If we look at the tax savings we have created with these three simple techniques, Jack and Jane have accomplished the following:

Technique #1	Tax savings of $1303 per year
Technique #2	Tax savings of $140 per year
Technique #3	Tax savings of $700 per year

Total tax savings   ***$2143***

If we look at the larger picture, the $2143 tax savings breaks down to $179 per month. Add that to the $650 of monthly cash flow due to debt service reduction and Jack and Jane have increased their monthly cash flow by $829. This will go a long way in helping to support a second child.

Jack and Jane could also choose to fund a 401K plan at work or start an IRA with the increased amount of money now available. This would, once again, reduce the tax obligation Jack and Jane currently have to pay. Remember, this does not even take into consideration the amount of state income taxes these techniques would save. If my brother-in-law would have come out of his consultation with his CPA with this game plan, he would have gotten his money's worth. I would say that Jack and Jane have begun to defend themselves quite nicely against the IRS. All this was accomplished by making some simple adjustments and implementing some basic strategies which are far too often overlooked.

Now let's move on to some of the more advanced tax planning techniques available for the Secret Millionaire.

Secret Millionaire Advanced Tax Planning Techniques

Obviously, there are more sophisticated techniques that wealthy taxpayers use to combat their high tax burden. And like I said before, if these techniques work for the big boys, they can work for you as well.

> *...if these techniques work for the big boys, they can work for you as well.*

The most common and beneficial tax strategy available today is to start your own business. Let me say that another way, the greatest tax shelter available today is to own and operate your own business. I have heard it said many times, "If you are not self-employed, do whatever it takes to get that way." Remember, starting your own business is not as difficult as you may think. You can start your own business while keeping the job you have now. I have seen businesses started in virtually every capacity, real estate businesses, stock trading businesses, consulting businesses, multi-level marketing businesses, independent travel agent businesses, and many, many more. Whatever it is that you decide you want to do as your business, the key is to get things started. This point is so important that it bears repeating: ***Owning and operating your own small business is the greatest tax shelter available today.***

While the primary goal of running a business is to support your family and your lifestyle, a very attainable secondary goal is to provide tax benefits to those who own the business. Now you may make your living at your nine to five job, but nothing says you can't start a business to enjoy some of the many tax benefits that owning a business brings to the table. The next few chapters of this book are dedicated to running your own business and the different types

of business structures available to help you achieve your goals. Remember, the Secret Millionaire concept is dedicated to estate planning, asset protection, and tax reduction. Forming your own business with the use of business entities can help accomplish all three goals. Let's take a look at some of the many tax benefits available for small businesses.

Secret Millionaire Tax Magic

I believe we need to clarify exactly why you need to start your own business. Starting your own business can help people who have serious tax problems. The simple truth is, starting your own business can help you regardless of your tax situation. Let's take a closer look at how this can help you with your particular tax scenario.

In this country, we all must pay taxes on our income. That is the case whether we operate as individuals, as sole proprietorships, as partnerships, or any other type of business entity. The key is to learn to handle these taxes in the best way possible. There are certain expenses which we all must pay. The trick is to use "before tax" dollars on these items rather than "after tax" dollars. Specifically, we need to find a way to deduct these items from our gross income. But what expenses are deductible? Let's get into this topic so that we can start reducing our tax bills.

What is deductible to me if I start my own business?

I am not the type who feels that it is necessary to memorize all of the tax code sections, but I do believe that there are certain tax code provisions which are essential to your success. Section 162 of the IRC is one of those sections.

Basically, it is the cornerstone for determining which business expenses are deductible. The section is so important to your overall success that I wanted to include the initial portion. Section 162 says:

"Internal Revenue Code section 162 'Trade or business expenses.'
  (a) In general. There shall be allowed as a deduction all the ordinary and necessary expenses paid or incurred during the taxable year in carrying on any trade or business, including
  (1) a reasoable allowance for salaries or other compensation for personal services actually rendered;
  (2) traveling expenses (including amounts expended for meals and lodging other than amounts which are lavish or extravagant under the circumstances) while away from home in the pursuit of a trade or business; and
  (3) rentals or other payments required to be made as a condition to the continued use or possession, for purposes of the trade or business, of property to which the taxpayer has not taken or is not taking title or in which he has no equity."

Many times, legitimate business expenses are quite obvious. In some cases, such as expenses associated with traveling, the IRS provides specific instructions for determining what is "ordinary and necessary." This is done through published income tax "regulations." These regulations are very important and as such, you should familiarize yourself with them or develop a relationship with a tax advisor who is familiar with them. If you are looking for a good tax advisor and do not necessarily insist on having one in your own area, feel free to call our offices and speak with one of our tax professionals at 1.877.868.9742. You will find that calling and speaking with one of our tax

pros doesn't cost, it pays.

Nowhere does the tax code specifically define the terms "ordinary and necessary." Instead, federal courts have tried to determine what Congress intended with this language and have tried to apply it to a particular set of facts.
"Ordinary" has been held by courts to mean "normal, common and accepted
under the circumstances by the business community." "Necessary" means
"appropriate and helpful." By looking at these two together, it appears that
"ordinary and necessary" refers to the purpose for which an expense is made.
For example, renting office space seems like one of the most ordinary and
necessary expenses you could possibly incur in your business. However, it is
neither ordinary nor necessary if it is not actually used in running your business.

The term "ordinary and necessary" is really quite vague. Given this vague-
ness, it's not surprising that many business people have tried to push things.
Unfortunately, the IRS has pushed back. A compromise is sometimes reached,
and sometimes the issue is even thrown into a court's lap. The court's determination then becomes a precedent for future decisions.

One way that people will try to push things a little too far is by paying exorbitant amounts for items so that they can receive an exorbitant tax deduction.
The IRS knows that people don't intentionally overpay for anything. For this
reason, amounts paid aren't usually questioned. However, auditors do sometimes object to expenditures they deem to be unreasonably large. While the
tax code itself contains no limitation on what is considered too large of an
expense, courts have ruled that it is inherent in IRC 162. Outrageous amounts
fall outside of the "ordinary and necessary" parameters.

The biggest concern of the IRS when auditing business deductions is whether purely personal expenditures are being claimed as business. The IRS keeps a close eye on this since business people regularly try it. The good news is that you can often arrange your affairs legally in a way that lets you derive considerable personal benefit and enjoyment from business expenditures. The most important thing is to understand what you can and cannot do.

One of the best pieces of advice I could possibly give you is to be careful if you deal with relatives. The IRS will probably be suspicious about expenses paid to a family member, or to another business in which your relatives have an ownership interest. In tax code parlance, these are termed "related parties." An IRS auditor may suspect that profits are being taken out of your business for direct or indirect personal benefit under the auspices of business expenses when actually the person is merely trying to evade taxes.

When studying tax information, it is important to note that tax rules cover not only what expenses can be deducted but also *when* they can be deducted. As discussed earlier, certain expenses are deductible in the year they are incurred, while others must be taken over a number of years.
The first category is called "current" expenses. Current expenses are generally everyday costs of keeping your business going, such as the rent and electricity bills. The tax rules for deducting current expenses are fairly straightforward; you subtract the amounts spent from your business's gross income in the year the expense was incurred.

The second category is "capitalized" expenditures. These expenditures are made to generate revenue in future years. These are "capitalized". What this means is that they become assets of the business. As these assets are used,

their cost is attributed to the revenue they help earn. This is allows the business to more clearly account for its true profitability from year to year.

The tricky part is to know what is a current expense and what is a capital expense. Normal repair costs, such as fixing a broken copy machine or a door, can be deducted in the year incurred. The cost of making improvements to a business asset must be capitalized if the enhancement:

a)   adds to its value, or
b)   appreciably lengthens the time you can use it, or
c)   adapts it to a different use.

"Improvements" are usually associated with real estate. Costs for items with a "useful life" of one year or longer cannot be deducted in the same way as current expenses. These costs are treated as investments in your business, and must be deducted over a number of years. The deduction is usually called *depreciation*. There are many rules for how different types of assets must be depreciated.

The tax code lays out limits on depreciation deductions. These limits cover how many future years a business must spread its depreciation deductions for asset purchases. It is important to note that all businesses, large and small, are affected by these provisions. (IRC 167, 168, and 179.) If you wish to obtain copies of these codes, contact the IRS at www.ustreas.gov.

A valuable tax break creating an exception to the long term write-off rules is found in IRC 179. A small business owner can write off in one year most types of its capital expenditures up to a grand total of $19,000. It is important

to note however, that this amount will be gradually increased to $25,000 over the next few years. Businesses should take full advantage of this provision every year. This is what is oftentimes referred to as "asset expensing."

One thing you must realize is that different items are treated differently. Some common and not-so-common business expenses have special rules that govern how they must be tax deducted. One of the most common refers to the deductibility of automobiles.

Automobile Expenses

A common corporate perk for many small businesses has always been the use of a company car. In particular, outside sales people have come to expect this as part of their compensation package.

However, more and more companies are allowing employees to drive their own cars because they can eliminate a lot of internal paperwork and have less trouble with the IRS at tax time. The reason is, most employees use their company car for personal use, anyway, as well as their business purposes. Employers then have to keep track of all of the personal use and treat it as taxable income to the employee. That produces additional paperwork and a record keeping nightmare.

To eliminate much of that record keeping and the significant tax liability that results, a corporation can just give a car to an employee. That means that you can write off the cost of any car your corporation gives to an employee, including yourself. Mileage accumulation is eliminated as a factor for tax reporting purposes, as is the difference between business to personal mileage.

Any employee personal use is just considered a compensation expense.
Then, by requiring employees to use their own vehicles and reimbursing them
for their expenses, your corporation can reduce those annoying paperwork
requirements even further. If you are planning to do this, your corporation
should adopt a standard procedure requiring employees to submit expense
account forms regularly which detail specific mileage usage on behalf of the
business, either weekly or monthly.

The IRS treats such reimbursements as a wash. The corporation does not
show the reimbursement as taxable income to its employees and employees
are not required to keep or provide records of expenses on their tax returns.
Any employee who requires additional reimbursement can attempt to deduct
them on Form 2106, "Employee Business Expenses," and that money is treated
as a miscellaneous itemized expense.

You may choose to set up a reimbursement plan for your corporation that is
not based on the standard, so many cents-per-mile method. You could, for
example, pay a flat rate to your employees that you have determined over
time is a fair compensation for using their own vehicles for company business
(including your own, of course.) Or, you could combine a flat rate, say $250
a month, with a reduced per-mile rate. These plans require more record
keeping on your part, but they also reduce the risk of having problems with
the IRS down the road.

Now, since the use of a company owned car is considered a taxable fringe
benefit, the value of the personal use is subject to federal income and state
unemployment taxes. This requires your corporation to put a dollar amount
on the value of the personal usage. There are a couple of ways to go about

this.

You can consult the lease tables in IRS Publication 535 to learn the lease value of any vehicle. If your employees only use their cars part of the year, you can use the daily value listed in Publication 535, or a value can be prorated for any portion of the year. Using records submitted by the employee, you must then determine the percentage of time the employee drives the car on personal business. To obtain a copy of Publication 535, contact the IRS at 1.800.TAXFORM or visit them on the web at www.ustreas.gov.

Next, calculate the personal value of the car by multiplying the percentage of personal use by the annual lease value of the car. On a vehicle driven 10,000 miles per year, which an employee shows he uses 15% of the time on personal business, then 1,500 miles become personal miles. Assuming that a vehicle has an annual lease value of $3,600, 20% of that, or $720, is taxable income to the employee that drives it.

An employee can then be reimbursed for either the actual cost of gasoline or a standard $.055 per mile. So, if the employee has been reimbursed $550 (10,000 miles x .055) for gas for the year, he would have to include that in his gross income, which he could offset with an itemized deduction for gas expenses.

The other method that your company can use is the standard mileage rate of $.325 per mile to figure the value of personal use on the vehicle. In the previous example, that 1,500 personal miles would be reported as $487.50 of taxable income.

THE SECRET
MILLIONAIRE

It is advisable to seek the assistance of a qualified tax professional in determining exactly what type of method you should implement.

Your corporation will have several choices on how you withhold taxes on the taxable income an employee draws due to the use of a company car. You can either withhold using the flat 20% rate or adopt the normal withholding method for supplemental wages. Either way is fine, provided you are consistent.

Another option is to not withhold anything. But you must notify your employees before January 21 of a given tax year (or within 30 days of providing the car) so they have a chance to change their W-4's. You want them to be able to hold back additional withholding from their paychecks to cover any additional taxes. Your company will also be responsible for Social Security and unemployment taxes on the value of a company car for some employees in the higher income brackets.

One of the big tax savings for you and your corporation is the ability to purchase a new luxury car each year at a relatively small cost. For purposes of this example, let's say the vehicle you buy costs $40,000. The tax law considers the additional compensation that you have received to be equivalent to the interest you would have had to pay to your corporation on the loan for the car.

In other words, you are paying the interest on the loan with the extra compensation you are receiving. So, tax consequences become a wash. Although the compensation is still taxable, you get an offsetting deduction because the interest that you should be paying is deductible as long as the note doesn't exceed $100,000. Your corporation can also pay you 75% of the maximum

allowed first year depreciation on the business use portion of the vehicle. That amounts to $1,995 in this example, which is tax free to you and deductible by your corporation.

Next year, you can then sell that $40,000 vehicle for, say, $34,000, and use the proceeds plus an additional $6,000 out of pocket to pay off the loan to your corporation. What then? Repeat the process, of course. This strategy can allow you to drive a new $40,000 car every year at a net cost to you of around $4,000 per year ($6,000 out of pocket minus the depreciation.)

Education Expenses

One question which always comes up in our seminars and in our meetings with clients, is whether education expenses are deductible. The rule of thumb is that you can deduct education expenses if they are related to your current business, trade or occupation. For these expenses to be deductible, the tax code requires that an education expense must either be:

a)   to maintain or improve skills required in your (present) employment, or

b)   required by your employer or as a legal requirement of your job or profession.

Let me add one caveat here. Education expenses that qualify you for a new job or business are not deductible under the tax code. This tax rule has been interpreted rather narrowly by the IRS and courts. For this reason, it is advisable to consult a tax advisor before you deduct these expenses.

Travel Expenses

Travel expenses are those incurred by employees while traveling away from home, including their meals and lodging. The IRS makes a clear distinction between "travel" expenses and "transportation" expenses. Transportation expenses include only the actual costs of travel which are incurred in the conduct of business while the employee is *not* away from home. Meals and lodging are not included in such expenses.

For example, if you lived in Dallas, but were assigned to work in Denver, you couldn't deduct any of the expenses for traveling, meals or lodging in Denver since that is your *tax* home of record. Going home to Dallas over a weekend, in this case, would not be considered "for business purposes" by the IRS.

"Home" is clearly defined for travel purposes by the IRS as a taxpayer's place of business, employment station, or post of duty, no matter where the taxpayer actually lives. Corporate "travel" and "transportation" expenses are both deductible, but they must be separated for IRS reporting purposes.

So, what are deductible travel expenses? The following are considered to be normal and necessary travel deductions:

     1) Any "common carrier" fares (air, bus, rail, boat, taxi, etc.)

     2) Baggage charges

     3) Meals and lodging (either en route to or at the destination)

4) Rental or maintenance of an automobile

5) Reasonable cleaning and laundry expenses

6) Telephone, telegraph, computer or fax expenses

7) Cost of transporting sample cases or display materials

8) Cost of display or conference rooms

9) Cost of maintaining and operating an airplane

10) Cost of secretarial help

11) Tips paid incident to any of the above expenses (within reason)

12) Other miscellaneous expenses related to travel

Full deductibility is allowed by the IRS for all travel expenses incurred while looking after income-producing property, including travel to consult with investment advisors and brokers. In most cases, stockholders are not allowed to deduct the cost of travel expenses to attend stockholder meetings of companies in which they own shares.

Travel costs incurred traveling out of the United States to establish new foreign markets for existing products may be deducted as long as such expenses are reasonable and necessary. Lavish and extravagant expenditures are not

deductible. (Note what does not qualify under foreign travel below.)

Travel and transportation expenses incurred while looking for employment in the same line of work are fully deductible. However, any payments made by a prospective employer as inducement to accept their employment is considered income and must be reported.

There are several kinds of travel expenses that do not qualify as IRS deductible expenses. For example, if you travel away from home, but do not stay overnight, the IRS has ruled that you cannot deduct meals and lodging. This ruling has even been upheld by the Supreme Court. So "per diem" payments you receive in such situations must be reported as income.

If you travel with your spouse, most costs for the spouse are not deductible unless you can establish that your spouse's presence served a bona fide business purpose. Deductions have been allowed by the IRS in situations where a taxpayer could prove that a spouse's presence was considered important for the company's public image.

If you are traveling in the U.S., and your trip consists of both business and personal pursuits, the IRS has ruled that you cannot deduct the costs associated with the trip unless there is *clear evidence* that the primary nature of the trip is related directly to your trade or business. In many cases, expenses incurred at your destination which are properly associated with your trade or business are deductible even though the travel to and from the destination are not. In other words, if you travel to a resort to close a business deal, but spend a day on the slopes skiing afterward, the travel *to* and *from* the resort may not be deductible, but the expenses incurred while actually doing busi-

ness *can* be. Every situation is different in the eyes of the IRS. Keep that in mind.

Now, if you travel outside the U.S. for primarily business purposes, but there are some non-business activities done in the process, the cost of travel from home to the place of business and back *may* not be deductible by an individual. The cost may have to be allocated between business and non-business activities, unless any *one* of the following tests is relevant:

    1) Travel outside the United States is for a week or less;

    2) Employee is not related to an employer and are not managing executives;

    3) Employee had little control over making trip arrangements;

    4) Less than 25% of the time outside the U.S. is spent on personal activity; or

    5) Vacation time was not a consideration in scheduling the trip.

Costs for travel related to educational purposes are not normally deductible, either, unless such travel is necessary to engage in activities that are designed to promote deductible education. For example, a Russian language teacher is not allowed to deduct the expense of going to Moscow on vacation simply to improve his or her knowledge of Russian culture and language. But, if the same teacher were to conduct an educational tour for high school students through the Russian countryside, those expenses might be considered deduct-

ible since the teacher incurred them while educating students, which is a language teacher's primary trade.

In order to deduct registration fees or travel and transportation costs associated with attending conventions, seminars or trade shows, you *must* be prepared to prove to the IRS that such income-producing purposes are directly related to your trade or business. Typically, the expenses incurred in connection with financial planning or investment seminars and meetings are not allowable deductions.

For travel expenses incurred while identifying a new domestic location for an established business, or for expenses incurred while trying to go into a new business, no deductible expense is allowed. Such travel expenses must, instead, be capitalized into the cost of the new property.

To get around this problem, you may want to take a personal deduction for all of your costs. Then set up a new corporation for the specific purpose of identifying a new location and follow the rules for treating its stock as Section 1244 stock. Then purchase the stock from the corporation in the amount you expect the search is going to cost. Have the corporation take on the expenses for the search, then if you don't find a good location, you can liquidate the corporation and take your losses as an ordinary deduction instead of a capital loss.

For deductible travel expenses, taxpayers must provide evidence of the following elements to support their deductions:

1) The separate amount of each expenditure

2) Dates of departure and return home for each trip

3) The travel destination for each portion of each trip

4) Reason for the travel, or the expected business benefit derived

Legal and Other Professional Fees

From time to time you will need to seek the assistance of professionals. Professional fees for attorneys, tax professionals, or other consultants generally can be deducted in the year incurred. For instance, fees for forming the business are immediately deductible. On the other hand, when professional fees clearly relate to benefits which will be received in future years, they must be deducted over the life of the benefit. Some fees fall into a gray area. For these types of fees, you can choose between deducting them all in the first year or spreading them over future years. This is a decision you should make with the assistance of your tax advisor.

Speaking of your tax advisor, I have some good news for you. Tax assistance is fully deductible. Many times, business people want tax advice covering both their business and individual taxes. Oftentimes, these are interwoven. For instance, you might ask your tax advisor how to minimize taxes on all of your income from all sources. Her fee qualifies as a business tax deduction in proportion to the *business* advice given. The remaining portion can also be deducted, but as a personal itemized deduction on Schedule A of your personal return. This is another expense which should be run by your tax accountant.

Entertainment Expenses

One of the biggest arguments in corporate expense meetings is invariably, "Who can be entertained by the business and be considered as a legitimate write off?" You might be surprised to learn that the IRS has no specific list of the kind of people who can or cannot be entertained. IRC regulations indicate that it almost always depends on the circumstances of a particular situation. Typically, any customer, supplier, employee of a client, agent, partner, or professional advisor can be entertained, whether they are established or prospective.

Entertainment costs for these people must be ordinary and necessary for carrying on the trade or business, and are not deductible unless business is discussed before, during, or after a meal, or the meal is "directly related" to, or "associated with," the conduct of business.

The deduction is limited to fifty percent of the actual cost, as long as such cost is not determined to be lavish or extravagant. The only exceptions to the fifty percent rule are expenses that fall in the following categories:

1) Employer paid recreation for a company picnic, holiday party, etc.

2) Minor fringe benefits including such things as holiday gifts, etc.

3) Any amount treated as compensation to the recipients, whether they are employees or not

4) Promotional samples and materials made available to the public

5) Tickets to charitable sporting events, to the extent such ex
penses meets three conditions:

>   (a) the event's primary purpose is to benefit a qualified
>   non-profit organization;
>   (b) the entire net proceeds go to the charity; and
>   (c) the event uses volunteers to perform the event's work.

IRC rules cover the entire cost of the event, including parking and meals, and are often used to deduct the cost of such things as charity golf tournaments and other sports outings.

You need to be careful with (5) above, as deductions taken at what the tax code describes as "entertainment facilities" are usually disallowed. Places like ski lodges, hunting lodges, yachts, swimming pools, beach houses, hotel suites, or other housing located in recreational areas are red flags on most IRS reports. Even dues paid to social and athletic clubs are no longer determined to be "ordinary and necessary" expenses to the extent that the club is used as a source of valuable business contacts.

The giving of business "gifts" is another gray area for most corporations. What can you write off, and what can't you? The IRS code has simplified this question considerably. Expenses for ordinary and necessary business gifts are deductible to the extent they do not exceed $25 in a year to any one person. The $25 limitation does not apply to items that cost less than $4 and

have the giver's name permanently imprinted, all obvious promotional materi-
als, or any item awarded to an employee because of length of service, productivity, or safety achievements (that do not cost more than $400).

For deductible entertainment expenses, in addition to the above information,
taxpayers must provide evidence of the following elements to support their
deduction:

    1) Name, address, or location of the place of entertainment

    2) The type of entertainment if that is not apparent by the name

    3) Purpose for expense, or the expected benefit derived for busi-
       ness

    4) Occupation, title, name, and other designation to establish the
       business relationship of the persons entertained to the tax
       payer

To make sure you don't encounter problems with the IRS with these
deductibles, employees should keep a detailed expense diary on a timely basis that clearly delineates all of the above information. This should be itemized
carefully and kept as current as possible. It is also very important to keep all
receipts on file for at least three years from the date of filing an income tax
return on which any such deductions were claimed.

Reimbursements

An "accountable plan" is a reporting method that qualifies under rules on what the IRS will accept as a reimbursement arrangement for business expenses incurred by employees. The difference between a properly documented accountable plan and a "non-accountable plan" can mean significant tax savings to you and your employees.

If your plan is accountable, your corporation does not report its reimbursements to employees as income. The reimbursements and the employees' expenses are considered trade outs by the IRS, and thus do not have to be included in anyone's income.

Under a non-accountable plan, though, reimbursements must be included as part of the income that employees' report on their W-2's. Such reimbursements (since they are considered income) must also have income taxes, unemployment taxes, and Social Security taxes withheld on them. That means more work for your corporation's accounting department.

Employees then have to deduct all business expenses on their tax returns as miscellaneous itemized deductions. These expenses are only deductible to the extent that they exceed two percent of adjusted gross income. This usually results in a situation where the additional income exceeds the deductions and the employee ends up owing additional taxes. If you happen to be both a shareholder of the corporation and an employee, this means you get taxed *twice* on the same income. The corporation incurs additional employment taxes, and you incur additional personal income taxes.

The IRS requires that such reimbursements meet three requirements:

1) Reimbursements must have a direct business connection.

2) Expenses must be properly substantiated.

3) Excess reimbursements must be returned to the corporation.

ITEM (1) Deductible reimbursements must be directly related to expenses incurred by an employee while conducting business for the employer. Such reimbursements can be paid in advance to prevent employees from having to use their own personal money for anticipated expenses, or can be paid in regular increments (per diem, etc.) to employees who have regular entertainment or travel expenses.

It is not a good policy to provide advances to employees for expenses when they aren't expected to incur such expenses right way. The IRS has ruled in such cases that the money should be counted as income to the employee at the time it was paid. It is also a really good idea to repay all reimbursements to employees with separate checks that identify the payment as such. You always want to keep wage payments and records as separate and distinct as possible from reimbursable expense payments.

ITEM (2) The IRS regulations are quite specific about what is and is not deductible, and virtually every reimbursement item must be substantiated by a specific type of record. Personal recollection, or rule-of-thumb ("That's how we've always done it,") policies are not considered adequate reporting methods.

Almost every expense that would normally be incurred in the course of business (yes, that makes for a lot of rules) has special substantiation rules in-

cluded in the tax code. The rules require that employees provide their employer with proof of the expense, including a time, place, and business purpose. When an employee has expenses that are not covered under IRS rules, the corporation is expected to get information that enables it to identify the nature of each expense and conclude that such expenses are substantiated before reporting them one way or another.

ITEM (3) Accountable plans require employees to return any and all amounts that exceed the substantiated expenses. Corporations should never pay money in advance more than 30 days before an anticipated expense is incurred, and employees should provide substantiation no longer than 60 days afterward and then provide any returns of excess payment within at least 120 days. Employers should provide employees with a detailed expense account report once per calendar quarter to allow them to substantiate or return any excess expense amounts.

Medical Expenses

A major consideration for corporations these days is medical care for employees and other associated medical expenses. The IRC is quite explicit on what can be deducted in this area. For most situations, 100% of all of the following medical expenses can be deducted:

1) Accident & health insurance
2) Acupuncture
3) Adoption
4) Air conditioner (for allergy relief or other medical condition)
5) Alcoholism treatment

6) Ambulance costs

7) Birth control pills

8) Blind person's attendant (to accompany student, etc.)

9) Braille books and magazines, seeing-eye dogs, or any special education and/or educational aids for the blind

10) Capital expenditures (or home modifications for handicapped individuals, primary purpose medical care)

11) Car or van equipped to accommodate wheelchair passengers, including handicapped controls

12) Childbirth preparation classes for expectant parents

13) Chiropractors

14) Christian Science treatment

15) Clarinet & lessons (to alleviate severe teeth malocclusion)

16) Computer data bank, storage and retrieval of medical records

17) Contact lenses

18) Contraceptives

19) Cosmetic surgery

20) Crutches

21) Deaf person's hearing aids (hearing aid animals, lip-reading expenses, note taker for deaf student, computer modifications, etc.)

22) Dental fees

23) Dentures

24) Doctor's fees

25) Domestic aid

26) Drug addiction recovery

27) Drugs and prescriptions

28) Dyslexia language training

29) Electrolysis

30) Elevator to alleviate cardiac condition

31) Eye examination and prescription glasses

32) Hair transplants

33) Halfway houses (drug, alcohol rehabilitation, etc.)

34) Health club dues prescribed by physician for medical condition

35) Health Maintenance Organization (HMO)

36) Hospital care

37) Hospital services (outpatient)

38) Indian medicine man (Native Americans)

39) Insulin

40) Iron lungs

41) Laboratory fees

42) Lead paint removal

43) Legal expenses (authorization for treatment, etc.)

44) Lifetime medical care

45) Limbs (artificial)

46) Mattresses (prescribed to alleviate arthritis, etc.)

47) Nursing homes

48) Nursing Services

49) Obstetrical Expenses

50) Operations

51) Orthopedic shoes

52) Osteopaths

53) Oxygen equipment

54) Patterning exercises for handicapped children

55) Prosthesis

56) Psychiatric care

57) Psychologists

58) Psychotherapists

59) Reclining chairs for cardiac patients

60) Remedial reading schools (special education or handicapped)

61) Sexual dysfunction

62) Sterilization operations

63) Swimming pool (for treatment of polio or arthritis, etc.)

64) Taxicab to doctor's office

65) Telephones, equipped for deaf persons

66) Televisions (close captioned decoders, etc.)

67) Transplants

68) Vasectomies

69) Vitamins

70) Wheel chairs

71) Wigs (for alleviation of physical or mental discomfort)

72) X-Rays

The following is a short list of other assorted expenses allowed to corporations. Within IRS guidelines, most corporations are allowed to deduct 100% of the following expenses:

1) Advertising expenses

2) Auto expenses

3) Awards

4) Cleaning expenses

5) Depreciation and Section 179 expenses

6) Convention expenses

7) Delivery expenses

8) Dues and publication expenses

9) Foreign conventions

10) Gas and oil expenses

11) Insurance expenses

12) Legal and professional expenses

13) License fees

14) Mailer expenses

15) Meals on premises expenses

16) Office expenses

17) Pension expenses

18) Per diem meals, including incidental expenses

19) Per diem lodging, including incidental expenses

20) Postage and freight expenses

21) Trade shows and conference expenses

22) Tax expenses (including payroll, property, sales, etc.)

23) Utilities (phone, electric, gas, water, garbage, etc.)

SUMMARY

Depending upon your actual situation, there may be ways to significantly reduce your tax bill. Every individual and every company is different, and every situation is viewed differently by the IRS. Consult with a qualified tax attorney or accountant to make sure you are in compliance before assuming something is deductible. It is much better to not deduct an expense that you have doubts

> *Millionaires don't make money by hoping things will happen. They follow a pre-planned strategy to make things happen.*

about than to hope the IRS agrees with you. Hope is *not* a method! Million-aires don't make money by hoping things will happen. They follow a pre-planned strategy to ***make*** things happen. And that is what I want each of you to start doing today. Remember, first work on your individual tax situation and then move to the greatest tax shelter available; owning and operating your own small business. It is something that will put you well on your way to becoming a Secret Millionaire.

"Challenges can be stepping stones or stumbling blocks. It's all in your perspective."
Unknown

CHAPTER V
SECRET MILLIONAIRE TOOL #1: CORPORATIONS

S hould I form my own corporation? What will it help me to accomplish? How can it assist me with my particular situation? Should I do it now or later? Do you know the answer to these questions? If not, you better learn them.

These are but a few of the many questions I hear from people across the country when I speak to them about corporations. The decision to incorporate is one of the most important ones you will ever make. And it's one you must make in order to deal with the three areas that were covered in the previous chapters.

If you do not know the answers to those questions, rest assured that you are not alone. The fact is, most people do not know the answers. However, if they can't answer those simple questions, how on earth can they consider actually forming and operating a corporation? To many people, the thought of ever having their own corporation seems like a task far too complicated. As you will see, that is certainly not the case. It's not difficult, it's just different.

> *It's not difficult, it's just different.*

The key to answering the questions lies in gaining a full understanding of ex-

actly what it means to become incorporated. You must truly understand corporations before you decide to form one.

As you begin your endeavor of fully understanding legal entities and specifically for this chapter, corporations, I believe you must first begin with the absolute basics. While studying the basics may be quite elementary for some, it has proven to be essential in gaining an in depth comprehension of any topic, much less one as complex as a legal entity. Besides that, regardless of your level of experience, you can never get enough of the fundamentals.

Think about it. When you go to watch your favorite sports team play, when they practice before the game, are they practicing the difficult plays or the basics? The basics! If that is what the professionals do, perhaps you should take a hint and do the same thing. If you want to get the best results, you must do things in the best manner possible. Learn from those who are getting the results that you would like in your life. That is the secret applied by today's millionaires.

If you want to know about something, you first need to know what it is. With this in mind, you have to ask the most basic questions first. The most basic question to deal with when it comes to corporations is simply, "What is a corporation?" We will answer this question before going any further.

What is a corporation?

If you were to ask most people to define the term "corporation," I'm quite sure you would get a myriad of responses, none of which may be correct. I'm convinced, as I travel throughout the country speaking with individuals from

all walks of life, that there is a huge misconception out there as to exactly what it means to be incorporated.

Generally, the term conjures up images of New York City and the vast array of skyscrapers which serve as headquarters to the Fortune 500 companies. While these huge multinational companies may indeed be corporations, it must be realized that the corporation can also be the mom and pop grocery on your local street corner. It's also the real estate agency through which you purchased your home, the insurance agent you play golf with, and the restaurant where you have dinner.

Most people simply don't see these smaller businesses when they envision corporations. But in actuality, it is these smaller businesses that make up the bulk of corporations throughout the world. It is these smaller businesses which mean more to the average person when it comes to benefiting from the use of a corporation. In fact, it is these smaller businesses which belong to many of today's millionaires.

The typical corporation in this country is a small business. In many instances, this small business, this small *corporation*, is owned and operated by families and even friends. This seems strange to many people who tend to think of corporations more in terms of those companies whose shares are traded on Wall Street.

The fact is, the overwhelming vast majority of corporations in this country are privately held. Actually, of the thousands, even millions, of corporations currently operating in the United States, an extremely small number are publicly traded. The chances are, if you are reading this book with the thought of forming a corporation, you are not planning to form this type of publicly traded company. At least not yet, anyway.

This makes it a bit more difficult to explain to someone about corporations because much of what they know comes from what they have learned in conjunction with the stock market. It seems that people all too often tend to associate all corporations with the Dow Jones Industrials.

Really this comes as no surprise since a good knowledge of corporations can help one develop a greater understanding of how and why stock is traded on the various exchanges. Considering that some fifty million individuals have brokerage accounts, it is not hard to see why the primary understanding of corporations comes from this arena.

A slight familiarity with corporations is inherent in any investment and/or trading environment. To truly understand corporations, and, more importantly to understand how you can benefit by having a corporation, you need to set aside any preconceptions you have and look at corporations from a whole new perspective. If you can do this, it can mean money in your pocket!

Let's begin by looking at some of the legal definitions of a corporation. Then we'll break those definitions down into language that is more understandable and readily applicable to your daily life. One of the first steps in finding out what any legal term means is to look it up in a law dictionary. The most common dictionary, Black's Law Dictionary, defines a corporation as:

> An artificial person or legal entity created by or under authority of the laws of a state or nation, composed, in some rare instances, of a single person and his successors, being the

incumbents of a particular office, but ordinarily consisting of an association of numerous individuals, who subsist as a body politic under a special denomination, which is regarded in law as having a personality and existence distinct from that of its several members, and which is by the same authority, vested with the capacity of continuous succession, irrespective of changes in its membership, either in perpetuity or for a limited term of years, and of acting as a unit or single individual in matters relating to the common purpose of the association, within the scope of the powers and authorities conferred upon such bodies by law.

Dartmouth College v. Woodward, 17 U.S. (4 Wheat.) 518, 636, 657, 4 L.Ed. 629;
U.S. v. Trinidad Coal Co., 137 U.S. 160, 11 S.Ct. 57, 34 L.Ed. 640.

There it is. Now, does that clear everything up for you? That is the official definition of what it means to be a corporation straight from the Supreme Court. After reading this definition, I have a question for you: What is a corporation?

Seriously! I learned this lesson the hard way. Early on, when I was first studying to be an attorney, I met with a lady who wanted to know about a corporation. I did what I thought at the time to be the best thing which was to draft a memorandum outlining this legal definition of a corporation. Her response was certainly not what I expected but it taught me a valuable lesson. Her response was, "Everything I need to know about what it means to be a corporation is written right there in plain English but I still don't have a clue

what it means." Talk about an enlightening experience. I learned right then and there that people want real-world answers rather than a lot of technical legal jargon.

While this may be the legal definition of a corporation, it does little to shed light on the issue of what a corporation means to the average person. Too many times this is exactly the case. You can go to an attorney and the attorney can give you page after page of information on a subject and you leave the office more confused than you started, despite the fact that you actually have the "appropriate" documentation purportedly answering your questions. With this in mind, let's take a little different approach to defining exactly what it means to be a corporation.

Basically, a corporation is a separate and legal, artificial person. That's right, a separate person from you. The corporation is not you and you are not the corporation. It is completely separate; a distinct entity separate and apart from you. It has the same rights as a person but it is more of a legal entity than it is a person. This point needs further attention.

A corporation is a separate legal entity. It is an entity separate and apart from its members, stockholders, directors and officers. While it is indeed a separate entity, it is still dependent upon others in order to take any action. This is the best news of all.

That is great news for you because you are the person upon whom the corporation is dependent. The corporation can act only through its members, officers and directors or agents thereof. Although it is separate, the best part of this is that it can have no knowledge or belief on any subject independent of

the knowledge or belief of those who control the corporation. This works very well since you are going to be the person(s) in control. It can do nothing unless you tell it to.

You are in control over this entity in the same way that a parent is in control of their children (ideally). Some of you may be thinking that this is not necessarily a good thing. You may be thinking that you've got enough on your hands with your kids without having another one when you form your corporation. The difference is that the corporation always minds you, no matter what the situation. Wouldn't that be nice? Do you understand the power in that? Let's take a closer look.

The corporation is an artificial person. Its rights, duties and liabilities do not differ from those of a natural person under like conditions. The only difference between a corporation and those directing it is that it lacks the ability to think for itself. That is the purpose of the officers and directors. These individuals do the thinking for the corporation.

To evidence this fact, documentation is kept for all decisions made on behalf of the corporation in the form of minutes and/or corporate resolutions. These documents are crucial and will be discussed in later sections in much greater detail. This distinction between the entity and those who control it becomes key in determining exactly what it is that people are searching for when they make the decision to form a corporation.

This also leads to our next question which will really be a bit more telling in understanding what a corporation is all about. It often requires more information than a simple definition of an item before your mind can form a picture of

the item. The trick is to understand what that particular item does. What is the function that it performs which makes it of value to you? Knowing what it is that a corporation does will reveal more about the entity and why a person would want to have one.

For example, if someone asked you what a car is, you would be hard pressed to tell them what it is without telling them what it does. Just as you cannot truly understand what an automobile is without knowing what it does, so it is with a corporation. With this in mind, let's take a look at our next question: Why do people incorporate?

Why do people incorporate?

This is the question that really needs to be answered. If you can determine what makes a person decide that they would like to have a corporation, you can more accurately determine what a corporation is all about. Just like the automobile, you need to see why anyone would want this corporation.

As previously outlined, the corporation is an artificial, legal person. It is a citizen of the state wherein it is created. In a later chapter, we will look at the various jurisdictions where you may want to create your corporation. Right now, however, you need to understand that a corporation does not cease to be a citizen of the state in which it is incorporated by engaging in business in another state. Nor does it change its citizenship by acquiring property in another state. These are both great benefits of having a corporation.

Another incredible benefit of being incorporated is that the existence of that corporation is not affected by the death of a shareholder or by the transfer of

the shareholder's ownership stake (shares). This is phenomenal with respect to accomplishing estate planning objectives that must be addressed in any well thought out plan. Further, the corporation's existence is not affected in the event that one of its owners undergoes the unfortunate circumstances surrounding bankruptcy. This makes the entity excellent for asset protection.

The reason for this once again is because the corporation is separate. It is separate from its owners. It is separate from its officers and directors. It owns things in its own name, not in the name of the owners, officers, and/or directors. It is *separate*!

As a separate legal entity, a corporation has the same rights and characteristics that we all have. It is considered to have its domicile or home in the state in which it is incorporated

> *As a separate legal entity, a corporation has the same rights and characteristics that we all have.*

and the place where it retains its resident agent or home office in that state. When the corporation is physically located in a different place, the location of the corporation's resident agent is oftentimes referred to as its "statutory domicile." Considering the separate nature of corporations, let's take a look at some of the exciting possibilities presented for those who decide to incorporate.

The way I prefer to think of a corporation is that it functions as more of a twin brother or sister. Most of you have had days when you wished that you could send someone to work in your place so that you could stay home and do as you please. Really, wouldn't it be nice to have someone step into your shoes and deal with undesirable situations that you all too often find yourselves in? What if you had this other person that could fill in for you and all you have to

do is tell that other person what to do? You could do all of the thinking for that person so that he or she would know what to do for you. Wouldn't that be ideal? That is exactly what a corporation does.

You may be thinking to yourself, "Yeah, right, sounds like just a dream!" Today, you have all sorts of worries and concerns you have to deal with. It sounds almost too good to be true to think that you could have someone that could take care of that stuff for you. It would be great in today's litigious society to be able to associate assets with that other person rather than with yourself personally. Then that person could be sued rather than you, right? Would that be amazing or what? That is exactly how it works when you begin to understand things more fully.

As I explain the benefits of corporations to groups, this whole structure at first seems like a farfetched idea that simply doesn't exist. They think, "Too bad I can't send that person to court to risk his assets instead of mine. If only I really did have a person who would do anything I told him. I could have him hold title to those assets so that I could significantly limit my vulnerability to lawsuits in connection with those assets, giving me tremendous asset protection. In the event that the other person lost that lawsuit and a judgment was rendered against him, the worst that could possibly happen is that he would lose his assets, not mine. Best of all, my personal assets would not be attached." Sound pretty incredible? Actually, this is exactly what a corporation is all about.

The reason people decide to incorporate is to create a situation much like what I've just outlined. By setting up a corporation, it is as if you have formed a twin who has all the rights that you do, yet is completely separate and apart from you.

A corporation is indeed a legal person. It is an entity in and of itself with a life and an identity all its own. The corporation is not you and you are not the corporation. It is completely separate from you and under the law, it is treated as if it were a human being.

Basically, a corporation is a form of business entity which is created based upon the laws of a specific state or country. Corporations cannot be established simply by creating a document between parties. All corporations must be set up under the authority of the government of the jurisdiction in which they are created.

Which jurisdiction that will be is of great significance. So much so that we spend a good deal of time on it at our seminars and in our educational materials. If you are interested in obtaining further information on the benefits of Nevada corporations in particular, call Profit Publishing Group, Inc. toll-free at 877.868.9742. But right now, let's discuss an equally important aspect of corporations by answering another key question, when should one incorporate?

When should one incorporate?

A question of primary concern for many is exactly when they should form their corporation. This is certainly a good question, but it is not something that should be a hindrance to their plan. There are a great number of excellent reasons to place your activities within the corporate structure. The vast majority of these reasons are not time sensitive. The only real issue of a timely

nature would be the tax consequences. While we all understand that the tax laws change occasionally, the business value of forming a corporation stays constant.

The bottom line in determining whether it is time for you to establish your corporation is if you answer "yes" to any of the following questions:

1) Would you be interested in maintaining flexibility in the management and control of your own business?

2) Would you like to implement a plan whereby you could protect your assets?

3) Are you interested in maintaining privacy over your finances?

4) Do you want to lower your overall tax obligation?

5) Is preserving your estate for your heirs important to you?

If you answered "yes" to any of these questions, *now* is the time for you to form your corporation. One thing you need to understand is that this is contrary to what other professionals are advising out there. Many attorneys and accountants have a tendency to give the standard answer to the question of when to incorporate. It seems that they think they know the answer to your situation without ever really taking the time to hear about your situation. They just go on giving the same old standard answer. The fact is, the financial and legal environment in which we live simply will not allow for a "standard" answer to this question. Extraordinary results are not "standard".

There are several factors you must take into consideration in determining whether the time is right for you to incorporate. While this is not a decision to be made lightly, it is also not a decision you need to lose too much sleep over. Too many times, people will fret over their situation for so long that it turns out that the best time for them to have incorporated was a long time ago. The failure to take action may have cost them thousands, or even tens of thousands of dollars. If you are concerned about protecting your assets, planning your estate, or reducing your taxes, the time to take action is *right now*.

I never fail to be blown away by the responses I get from people who tell me about their dealings with so-called "experts" out there in setting up their business plans. These responses are amazingly short-sighted. Anyone who has dealt much with attorneys and/or accountants will recognize this frustration. I hear stories on a regular basis about how someone went for professional help and was told that they did not need a corporation until their income reached a certain dollar amount. Not only does this strike me as short-sighted, it is actually quite offensive to me as well.

The reason I find this so offensive is that it completely avoids the issue of asset protection. If one of these professionals says that you do not need a corporation unless you have at least a certain dollar amount, aren't they really saying that if you have below that dollar amount that your assets aren't worth protecting? This offends me! Every person reading this book has worked very hard to get where they are today. For a professional to say that what you've accomplished is not worth protecting is a slap in the face.

Really, if someone told you that you don't need a security system you would think that it must be because there is no need for one due to a low crime rate,

right? Does a new lawsuit being filed every thirty seconds sound like a low level? Think about it, if there was an epidemic in criminal activity and someone told you not to secure yourself, the only possible reason would be that they don't think that what you have is worthy of security. This is the advice that is often given out there.

If one of these professionals tells someone that they do not need a corporation until they reach a certain dollar amount, this tells me something about that advisor. It tells me that they have tunnel vision. They are not seeing the overall picture because they have focused all of their attention on just one issue, the money. Let me give you an example to illustrate my point.

I was teaching a seminar one night in Los Angeles and I had a member of the class tell me that their CPA told them that they did not need a corporation until they had at least fifty thousand dollars a year in income. The CPA said that the cost of the corporation would be more than the amount of money this individual would save in taxes for that year. According to that CPA, by the end of the year, after taxes were calculated and the cost of the corporation had been factored in, this person would end up paying one hundred dollars more to have the corporation. Let's take a closer look at this mentality.

It was true, as I understood after talking to this person, that he would end up paying more that first year if he set up a corporation. But my question for his CPA would have been, "What about next year? And the year after that? And the year after that?"

It seems that the CPA never really discussed that with his client. This was yet another example of where the CPA gave a true statement but one which was

little more than half a truth. Do you see what I mean about being short-sighted?

This sort of thing infuriates me about some attorneys and accountants who pass themselves off as financial experts. Let me point out right now in no uncertain terms that I highly recommend for you to build a Mastermind Team, which will consist of an attorney and accountant, to help you with your financial decisions. The point I make here is that you need to be careful in selecting that attorney and accountant. A CPA like the one I have mentioned can cost you a lot of money, and I don't mean just in fees. The worst part about it is that many people take their CPA's word as fact and stop right there.

There is a simple rule which I have learned in my life about how people judge others and their information. The rule is this. "If they are not up on it, they are down on it."

What I mean by that is that if your attorney or accountant is not up to speed on a particular subject, the chances are that they will not have anything particularly nice to say about it. If you hear them speaking negatively about something that you are interested in, the first thing you need to determine is how much they really know about that topic.

The best way to find out is to ask them, point blank. Many times, the problem is that they simply do not have the information, knowledge, or experience to comment on the subject but are afraid to let you know that. Call them on it. A good professional will answer your question, even if the answer is, "I don't know." It's worth a lot more for them to tell you they don't know, than to try to advise you by talking about something they know little about.

How can I use a corporation for asset protection?

Do the goals and objectives of asset protection cause you concern? Surprisingly enough, that's NOT the case with most folks. Many people feel that there is just no need for them to implement any protective measures because they have done nothing wrong and do not plan on doing anything wrong in their lives. Today, you need not do anything wrong to be taken to the cleaners in a lawsuit. All you have to do is *own* something.

Of all the reasons there are for incorporating, asset protection stands out above the others. With asset protection, you are implementing limited liability or protection for your personal assets and property in the event they are sought by creditors.

In today's society, everyone is faced with the potential threat of a devastating lawsuit. Now more than ever, you must have a plan to protect your assets. The corporation can help you immensely with this task. A corporation organized in the right place and operated in the right way can help you even more. This chapter will introduce you to key strategies to help you meet your objectives.

In this wildly litigious society, then, asset protection can be a great comfort. All you have to do is read the newspapers or watch television to see the nature of the legal nightmares that face property owners. The people of this country are more conversant in the concept of litigation than they have ever been in our history. It seems the solution to everyone's problem these days is to find someone to sue, and it doesn't matter whom, as long as they have assets to seize.

One major lawsuit in this kind of environment can completely wipe you out, if you are not properly protected. However, there are ways to make sure you are protected. You can avoid many of the risks of property ownership by implementing asset protection measures if you are just willing to do what it takes.

To accomplish that, all you need to do is take a pro-active stance in organizing your affairs. Today you hear of courtroom judgment amounts which completely and absolutely defy all logic. What you must realize more than anything else is this—it *can* happen to you!

Protecting your assets is completely legal, provided it's done right. Having stated that, I have to add a brief caveat, and coming from an attorney that's probably not too surprising for you. In structuring your overall affairs in a way which protects your assets, you *must* abide by the law. You cannot engage in illegal acts such as concealing assets, issuing false information or committing perjury.

The good news is that you can develop a solid and effective asset protection plan which is in full compliance with all the rules, regulations, and laws without doing anything wrong. The use of a corporation is the central element in that plan.

As you have already learned, when you create a corporation, you create a legal entity, effectively, a legal person. It is as if you have created a surrogate you. This new entity is now responsible for its own acts. The importance of this is that you are not individually responsible for the acts of this separate legal entity, unless you act fraudulently or criminally. In this event you can be sub-

ject to personal liability for your actions and all the repercussions that result. To prevent this, let's take a look at what constitutes fraudulent acts, so that you can make sure what you and your corporation are planning to do is not illegal.

When corporations lose a big lawsuit, there's always a desire to attempt to transfer some or all of the corporate assets to help keep them protected from creditors. But judgment creditors are just too smart to let most assets "slip through the cracks." And they have the courts on their side, armed with more technology now than ever before.

The law refers to this kind of illegal transfer of assets as a "fraudulent convey-ance," and it will almost always get you into hot water with the courts. The term is used to describe any attempt to improperly transfer assets to avoid lawsuits or the judgment awards that result. You must understand that, *"a conveyance for the purpose of avoiding collection of damages in a pend-ing action for a tort is fraudulent."* If you are concerned about whether or not a particular transfer that you are contemplating is fraudulent, consult with an attorney familiar with the law of fraudulent conveyance. My suggestion for finding such an attorney is to contact one specializing in bankruptcy law.

Fraudulent conveyance is based on the principal that creditors have a right of remedy against a debtor. If the court determines that a creditor's right to collect a viable debt is infringed due to transfer or conveyance of assets by the debtor, the debtor's entire transaction can be set aside.

Unfortunately, I can't give you a complete, proper and always applicable definition of fraudulent conveyance. The reason for that is because it changes

with each judge's interpretation, and is more often than not, based on specific circumstances. The courts rely on certain facts, like the length of time that separates a transfer of assets from an action that results in liability. That time can vary widely in different situations. There is no hard and fast rule.

However, The Uniform Fraudulent Conveyance Act (UFCA) is in effect in most states, and the Uniform Fraudulent Transfers Act (UFTA) is used in the remaining states. These two laws are virtually identical in the way they define two categories of fraudulent transfers. They are:

1) **Fraud in-law**: Also known as constructive fraud, this occurs when there is a gift or sale of a debtor's property for less than the fair market value. This must be done in the face of a known liability, which renders the debtor insolvent or unable to pay the creditor. Fraud-in-law can only exist when all the above elements exist. There is no need to prove that the debtor had *intended* to defraud the creditor.

2) **Fraud-in-fact**: Also know as actual fraud, this occurs when creditors prove that a debtor intended to hinder, delay or defraud them.

Transfers found to be fraudulent allow the court to force a retransfer of the assets to the creditors. Parties which receive the fraudulent transfer, and are deemed to be an innocent third party (unaware of the fraudulent intent) can place a lien against the transferred assets up to the amount that was paid for them in order to recoup their money.

Creditors have to act within a specific time frame to properly challenge a

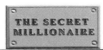

transfer done under fraudulent conveyance statutes. In most states, the statute of limitations is four years after the transfer is made or the debt is incurred,
or one year after it could have reasonably been discovered, whichever occurs
last.

In a federal bankruptcy case, the bankruptcy trustee usually has two years
from the first meeting of creditors to begin a fraudulent transfer claim. The
major exception to this is if the bankruptcy trustee chooses to bring fraudulent
transfer charges under state law instead. And believe me, you *do not* want a
federal bankruptcy trustee to file such charges.

How do you avoid this? Simple. Put a strategy in place before you have a
problem. Planning in advance gives your strategy a much better chance of
being upheld by a court.

The primary concept here is, that for any transfer of your corporate assets to
be protected, it needs to be supported by legitimate business reasons. Transfers must be made prior to any event or situation that results in a lawsuit.
Once an event has actually occurred, such transactions can be subject to
intense scrutiny. If a transfer of assets takes place *after* you have been served
with a lawsuit, it will be virtually impossible to justify the transaction as legitimate in the eyes of the law.

One thing for you to be aware of is that Nevada corporate law provides some
of the best liability protection there is for corporate officers and directors. But
knowledgeable directors should also insist upon indemnification by their corporation for any lawsuit brought against them resulting from their corporate
duties. To make this indemnification stronger still, the company should obtain

director liability insurance.

When corporations purchase this kind of insurance for their directors instead of having the individual directors purchase their own policies, defending claims becomes far less complicated, writing-off of the cost of premiums becomes less problematic, and the policies are usually far less expensive than individual policies would be.

Look for the following features in your director's insurance package:

1) What coverage does the policy provide? A good policy should have a minimum of a million dollars in coverage per occur rence. Larger corporations involved in high risk activity, such as public transportation or hazardous waste, will need a lot more.

2) What actions are excluded from coverage? Does the policy exclude claims based on fraud, dishonesty, libel, slander, se-curities violations, insider trading, or other such activities? These exclusions can often be negotiated back into your cover age at a higher premium.

3) What kinds of deductibles are there? Many policies use a "split deductible" approach to claims, where the policy only provides, say, 90% coverage and you pay the rest. On large judgments, though, even 10% can be a hefty amount of money. Some policies also have a flat deductible of $5,000 per direc-tor.

4) Will the company notify the directors if coverage is canceled?

5) Will supplemental insurance be provided that covers deductible lapses in coverage or exclusions?

The best way to avoid lawsuits, of course, is to keep your name off the corporate records in the first place. In Nevada, only the officers and directors are listed on any public records. That means if you can find someone else to act as a director, then your name doesn't have to appear on anything. This provides an added layer of privacy.

Nevada incorporating companies and/or resident agents can often provide "nominee" officers and directors for corporations that they are in the process of forming. Fees for this can range from a few hundred dollars a year up to a couple of thousand. If you're considering using such services, be sure you read the contracts because there are usually some additional costs for certain activities, such as excessive use of time.

To take things a step further in this strategy, and especially if confidentiality is a major priority for you, have your attorney hire the nominee officers on your behalf. The nominee officers and directors never need to know who you are, and if they take all their instructions from your attorney, that gives you additional protection because of the attorney-client privilege.

For professional people like physicians, dentists, architects, lawyers, and accountants, it is often a real struggle to find the right mix of tax breaks, liability protection, and corporate practicality under one corporate umbrella. As a result, many professionals use a professional corporation, which provides a

high degree of liability protection, as well as tax benefits specifically geared toward building a good pension plan. Unfortunately, even in well-organized professional corporations, professional people can still be held personally liable, regardless of their corporate status.

The solution to this problem is a strategy that was designed especially for a medical practice. This is how it works:

1) The professional sets up a professional corporation through which the professional service is performed.

2) A second, regular business corporation is formed for the purpose of managing the practice, and which will also own the client base.

3) The stock of the business corporation is issued to the professional's spouse as his or her separate property. (An option would be to issue the stock to an irrevocable trust as described earlier.)

4) The business corporation hires the professional corporation, by contract, to provide the professional service in return for a set annual fee. *If you do this, be sure to have a contract drafted which outlines the specific terms of the agreement.*

5) The client, or patient, pays the business corporation, which handles the billing, for all services rendered.

This strategy ensures liability protection by separating the risk associated with the professional service's efforts from the real assets of the business. If the professional is hit with a judgment in court, the business corporation could then exercise a provision in the contract between the two companies that allows it to, in essence, *fire* the professional corporation and replace it with another professional service provider. And the real asset, the professional person's skill, can then be transferred to a new entity with relatively little trouble. Then the process is repeated. In the event that you decide to implement this strategy, you should seek the assistance of a qualified attorney specializing in this area.

How can the corporation help with estate planning?

At first, many people find it strange to be talking about a corporation as a way to take care of estate planning concerns. Some people consider estate planning to be the act of preparing for death, but it is not. It is the act of preparing for life for your assets after you are gone. It is the act of taking the worry out of your passing for those you care the most about—your children, your spouse and even your corporate partners.

One of the easiest and best ways to provide an estate plan for yourself and those important other people is to incorporate. A corporation can protect assets that would otherwise be difficult or impossible to liquidate under normal estate planning techniques.

A commercial operation, for example, could not easily be split up among two children and a spouse, but the profits from such an operation could be, provided those profits are funneled through a corporate entity. The corporation also provides a shield against taxes and other sources of disruption that could destroy a viable business, in the event of your death.

But the corporation's single biggest benefit to your estate planning strategies is its unlimited life span. Unlike people, corporations don't die of natural causes. Shareholder deaths do not, in and of themselves, cause the corporation to suffer. And at the same time, the corporation

> *...the corporation's single biggest benefit to your estate planning strategies is its unlimited life span.*

can absorb much of the shock of a major stockholder's death, provided that stockholder has put estate planning techniques in the forefront of corporate planning.

Here is another little "what-if" scenario for you to contemplate. I think it will demonstrate rather dramatically how estate planning can be a real blessing to you and your heirs.

Let's suppose that you decide to open a business and you wisely choose the Nevada corporation as the structure. You issue Class A Voting stock and Class B Non voting stock at the outset. Your total capital to start is $10,000, and of that amount, $1,000 is capitalized in exchange for Class A Voting stock and $9,000 is a loan to the corporation.

Now, you issue yourself some Class A stock, representing only 5% of the company. You then issue your spouse an equal 5% of Class A stock. You also issue 45% of the corporate stock to both of your children. However, they are issued Class B Non Voting stock instead of Class A.

That is a total of 100% of the corporate stock that has been issued, but you and your spouse still control the whole thing by virtue of issuing the two classes of stock. Even when your children get old enough to be responsible for their shares, they have no voting rights, so the corporation stays under your complete control.

Okay, so the corporation's business booms for the next 10 years and all of a sudden is worth $2 million. Unfortunately for you, a massive heart attack intervenes. This leaves your wife and children to cope with a myriad of legal problems, tax problems, creditor problems and liability problems, right? No, actually it doesn't. The corporation does business the day *after* you die just like it always has. And much of the weight of your death falls on the corporation instead of your family. But, having the solid foundation of Nevada corporate law, your corporation hardly even wavers.

Instead of your estate containing a business worth $2 million, which would leave the family with a massive federal estate tax bill of over half a million dollars, your estate only contains 5% of the $2 million business, or a paltry $100,000. Since the $100,000 value of your part of the business is well under the $625,000 lifetime exemption, your family will have no estate taxes to pay upon your death. You just saved your spouse and children from losing almost 25% of the worth of their company.

Do you feel good about what you accomplished for your family? Well, since you're a fictional fatality of the scenario, you probably won't know the difference. But your family certainly will. Now, let's take a look at some more million-dollar strategies for estate planning.

This next strategy uses the corporation and a limited partnership to transfer assets of enduring value to your heirs.

1) You have to form a corporation with No Par Stock, preferably in a corporate haven, such as Nevada. This corporation will exist solely as a "shell" having no assets, liabilities or value.

2) Once your corporation is set up, have the Board of Directors pass a resolution that sets a par value for corporate shares at a nominal amount, such as a penny per share.

3) Now you want to sell shares to your heirs at the price determined in the corporate resolution. Since they are purchasing the shares, the corporation is not being "gifted" to anyone, and there is no taxable event.

4) Next, you want to form a limited partnership for the purpose of owning the shares of the corporation. Give the partnership an extended life span, such as fifty years. The limited partnership agreement should provide for a termination of the partnership upon the death of the general partner. You become a 1% general partner and have the exclusive right to vote the shares of the corporation. The limited partners are your heirs.

5) Now, your heirs (the stockholders of the corporation) transfer their shares into the limited partnership in exchange for an ownership interest in the partnership. The general partner (you) owns 1%, you also own an additional 1% as a limited

partner, and your heirs become 98% limited partners.

6) It's time to sell your personal assets to the corporation for the lowest fair market value that you can defend. *(It would be a good idea to consult a tax advisor for this.)* Take back a demand promissory note with a long maturity period. The note should bear interest at a reasonable market rate, and can provide that in the event of your death, the corporation will for give any debt still owed.

7) Your corporation pays the interest as it becomes due under the note, providing you with some taxable interest income, but not a lot.

8) The end result is that, if you die, your heirs will already own any assets you intended to leave them.

This strategy can mean a great deal to both you and your family if properly implemented.

This next strategy will help minimize estate taxes on appreciating assets or on profits generated through a corporation by transferring capital gains taxes to an irrevocable trust.

1) First, you must form another Nevada corporate shell having no assets, liabilities, or value, just as before. You and your spouse can be the shareholders or you can go it alone. This corporation's purpose is to own appreciating assets, or to be

the beneficial party in a profitable business dealing.

2) Step two is to form an irrevocable trust, using an independent trustee, naming your heirs as the beneficiaries.

3) Now, you need to transfer the corporate shares into the trust under the $10,000 federal annual exclusion from estate and gift tax. Since the corporation is essentially worthless, this transfer triggers no taxable events, assuming you've made no other transfers that approach the $10,000 exclusion limitation. The trust now owns the corporation, and the Trustee controls the shares for the benefit of your heirs.

4) All appreciating assets you own should now be sold to the corporation for the lowest *defensible* fair market value, in ex change for a demand note bearing interest (similar to the lim-ited partnership strategy.) *Once again, it is advisable to con-sult with a qualified tax advisor to determine the appropriate amount.*

5) For a new business opportunity, the corporation is now able to entertain that business activity, since any value the enterprise builds will take place outside of your estate. Gains that occur will then be passed on to the trust automatically.

This is a strategy which can enable you to significantly minimize the estate taxes involved in your estate.

In a closely held corporation, the death of a major shareholder can cause some real problems unless you have a strategy in place to deal with this well in advance. These problems not only affect the estate of the shareholder, but can have serious ramifications as to whether the corporation can continue to operate or not. Here are a few of the problems a closely held corporation would face:

1) Creditors of the corporation can immediately pressure the company for early repayment of any loans, or impose additional restrictions or requirements on the company's operations until such loans are repaid.

2) Employees of the corporation may wonder if the corporation will be liquidated due to dissension between remaining share holders, or a lack of cash when creditor demands are placed on it.

3) Beneficiaries of the deceased shareholder may need money, which could induce the executor to make some kind of hasty distribution. That could put the deceased shareholder's executor in the position of having personal liability for unpaid taxes.

4) The deceased shareholder's estate will have the burden of proof in establishing the value of corporate shares. The IRS typically establishes as high a figure as possible for such stock, which the executor then has to dispute with fairly concrete proof. And that is not always possible.

One way around these problems is to have your corporation establish some sort of a buy-out agreement to protect against the loss of any key shareholders. The most popular form of a buy-out agreement is called a "buy-sell agreement" in which other stockholders agree to purchase, at a predetermined price, all of the shares of any party who dies.

After the death of a shareholder, remaining shares would be sold to the other shareholders who were parties under the buy-sell agreement. The value of the shares for estate tax purposes would set the price at the time of the transfer, because that price represents an actual sale at arm's length between two shareholders who couldn't know at the time they signed the agreement whether they would end up being purchasers or sellers of the stock.

In most cases, the IRS will honor the value of the deceased owner's shares under a viable buy-sell agreement if you follow these guidelines:

1) A valid buy-sell agreement must restrict stock transfers while the shareholder is alive. The corporation and/or the shareholders must have the right of first refusal on the transfer of shares, at the price specified in the agreement.

2) State a valid business reason for the buy-sell agreement. The IRS won't let you get away with buy-sell agreements that are designed solely to pass on corporate shares at less than full market value. However, the IRS does usually recognize that maintaining family control and ownership over a corporation is a valid business purpose for a buy-sell agreement.

THE SECRET
MILLIONAIRE

3) An *option* to buy or sell the stock is not sufficient for a valid buy-sell agreement. The deceased's estate must have an obligation to sell the shares at a specified price and, either the corporation or the shareholders must be obligated to purchase the shares.

4) The buy-sell agreement must not allow the number of shareholders to drop to a level where a personal holding company would result. This can happen if there is passive income involved or there are undistributed earnings present.

5) And last but not least, you must be reasonable. If you use a realistic method to set the value of shares, such as basing it on the earnings, or appraised value, etc., the IRS will agree with the value you set. Using a fixed price can create problems because the IRS knows that the real value of any corporation is likely to change over time.

What happens with a buy-sell agreement if no one has the funds to buy the outstanding shares when the time comes? The best way to eliminate that problem is to have each shareholder take out a life insurance policy on the other shareholders for this specific purpose. The policies could be assigned to a trustee to ensure that the proceeds will *only* be used to purchase shares from the estate. The insurance premiums won't be tax deductible, but any legal expense you incur to set up the plan and draft the agreement may be.

How can I use a corporation for tax reduction?

Now that you have your assets and estate protected by the corporation, the next strategy you need to learn is how to reduce those nasty taxes on it. Again, the strategies you are about to learn are perfectly legal as long as you follow the law. Remember, too, that we are talking about tax "avoidance" and not tax "evasion." Avoidance will reduce the amount of taxes you pay; evasion will reduce the amount of freedom you have.

Keep in mind that there are too many ways to significantly reduce your tax bill legally for you to ever consider operating illegally. If cheating on your taxes is your objective, this book is not for you. There is nothing creative in being dishonest. If you ever have a question between whether a particular tax strategy is an avoidance or an evasion, consult with a qualified tax accountant or advisor familiar with business taxation.

The toughest part of reaping financial benefits from a corporation these days is to take as much money out of the company as it can afford to pay you, while giving up the least amount of taxes to the government in the process. Owning your own business gives you the right to the money your corporation earns, but at the same time, the government has a right to take away some of your profits. Knowing how to legally avoid as much of that taxation as possible is a key strategy in building a viable plan. However, you have to be very careful how you go about putting that money in your pocket, otherwise you can seriously jeopardize the protection your corporate veil provides.

You've already learned that a Subchapter S corporation can go a long way toward reducing the negative tax consequences of double taxation to which

other kinds of corporations are subjected. So, what do you do about this double taxation? How do you keep the money without violating the law? The ideal solution would be to have your corporation spend the excess earnings in ways that benefit you and your employees, and still avoid having double taxation apply to it.

Here are some of the most effective methods for taking cash or benefits out of your company and still avoiding the problem of double taxation:

1) Salaries
2) Bonuses
3) Commissions
4) Loans
5) Leases
6) Employee benefit plans
7) Independent contractor fees for services
8) Fringe benefits and expense accounts

How do salaries help the corporation avoid taxes?

Setting salaries for owners or employees can be crucial in your efforts to avoid double taxation. Ideally, if you're threatened with double taxation you'll want to take out as much money in the form of salary as possible. That will likely make your personal income tax rate higher than you would like, but remember that salaries are deductible expenses for the corporation. How ever much money you receive in the form of salary, the corporation does not pay taxes on that amount and double taxation is at least reduced if not cut out altogether.

Once again, though, the IRS will have something to say about how you pay yourself. They will want to determine your importance to the business. If your role is determined to be "hands-on," (i.e. meeting with clients, coordinating activities, setting company goals and directions) then you can prove you have a personal impact on the entire operation of the business and are thus crucial to the company. But, if your work is "hands-off," and can be accomplished by someone else, your role might be considered less vital by the IRS and thus not worth the kind of salary you are paying yourself.

Whatever the case, the IRS will take a long, hard look at high salaries because if they can prove that the high salaries are there solely to avoid declaring dividends, they can make you pay more taxes. This is called a "Reasonableness Test," although it might be more appropriately called an "unreasonable test." The test applies a series of IRS standards to your compensation packages to determine if there are any disguised dividends built in anywhere.

Discretion plays a huge part in this testing process and is almost totally up to the IRS in most cases. So you need to pay particular attention to the following facets of the test to see just how they may apply to your situation.

The first thing the IRS looks at to justify your salary is the role you play in managing and directing your corporation's business. Many businesses are specialized or more complex than others, which may warrant significantly higher salaries across the board. In other words, the question becomes, "What would you be paid if you performed the same kind of specialized duties for some other business in the marketplace?"

If you can prove that you would be paid something similar to what you are currently making by another company, then you will likely have no trouble with the IRS over your salary. The best evidence here would be if you show that you have received an offer to run a similar company at a similar salary.

You can also find out what other people are being paid by consulting the statistics that state agencies provide on unemployment claims. Libraries, newspapers, classified ads, and industrial trade associations can also provide information to back up your claim. If that type of information is hard to come by for your type of work, then expert testimony is also accepted by the IRS.

The next test is how much time do you actually put in at your job? The IRS usually determines that executives who receive full time pay for part time work are receiving "disguised" dividends. Most of you real entrepreneurs who work 16 hour days won't have to worry about working too little, though. As long as you keep accurate records of your work days, you shouldn't have any trouble proving that you work full time.

The third test is, how does your background, experience and education relate to your work? The more specialized your training and experience, the higher you can justify your salary. Keep on file all of the educational credits, seminars, degrees, certificates, and achievements that relate to your work. Many of these things will be considered significant when or if the IRS evaluates your salary.

Next, the IRS will look at your corporation's history and present financial situation. They will want to determine if your compensation package, including any recent raises in pay, is appropriate for the size and kind of business

you are doing. Further, your salary will be looked at historically to see if it is in line with the company's past growth and profits. If these two determinations seem appropriate, the IRS should accept your salary and raises as justified.

In some cases, the tax man will want to know how much you earned in other jobs. Previous employment records are a good indicator of how much the corporation should have expected to pay you to secure your services. You can build a valid basis for your salary by showing a record of promotions and salary increases, even if they are from unrelated companies.

The IRS will always take into consideration the prevailing economic conditions when testing salary levels. Compensation is analyzed with the economic conditions in your particular industry in mind as well as the country as a whole. How the IRS compares your salary will depend to a large degree on whether the national economy and comparable corporations are enjoying prosperity or just struggling to survive.

How your salary fluctuates compared to other employees in your company when overall income is down is another major consideration for the IRS. If your company can afford to pay you a high salary when company income is reduced, you may have to explain the decision not to cut your own pay if you have had to cut salaries for others. This is easiest when you can show that employees who own no stock have continued to be paid by the company and have taken no pay cuts.

In some companies, salaries for managers are a function of a percentage of sales instead of a fixed amount. Computing executive salaries from sales is

perfectly acceptable to the IRS as long as the company does not raise that percentage in the middle of a year of high earnings. It is much less of a problem if you keep the percentage constant year around, allowing salaries to consistently rise or fall with sales.

The last things the IRS looks at are your company's dividend and bonus histories. By using close scrutiny of dividend and bonus practices over an extended period of time, the IRS often uncovers bonuses disguised as dividends. In particular, very low dividends paid to stockholders in years of very high bonuses are almost indefensible to the IRS.

Okay, now you know what the IRS tests are for salaries, but be careful here. Even if salaries look reasonable on the surface, certain practices can still raise red flags for illegal tax strategies. You need to structure your corporation so that the following situations will *not* present a problem:

1) Salaries alone are not the whole picture. The IRS is interested in your total compensation package. This includes all kinds of "perks" like pensions, profit sharing plans, insurance, and any company programs in which you participate. Company cars, boats, airplanes and other corporate "toys" are a factor, as are paid vacations and some forms of leisure travel. These all add to the value of your compensation package.

2) Stockholder salaries should never increase any faster than other high-level employees in the company. If stockholder salaries increase 20% during a period when other employees received raises of only 10%, then you can bet the IRS will be looking

for some disguised dividends.

3) Never use all of the company's earnings to pay salaries. If the combined salaries of shareholders leaves the company with minimal net earnings, the IRS may determine that the salaries represent disguised dividends. Net earnings should fluctuate right along with company income.

4) Shareholder salaries should never reflect a percentage of ownership. When salaries are proportionate to the amount of stock the officers hold, the IRS will almost certainly deem it as evidence that part of the salary is actually unpaid dividends.

5) By hiring family members to work for your company, you can keep income in the family at a lower tax rate than if it were earned by them as shareholders directly. As long as the work is actually being performed by family members, and their salaries are reasonable, the compensation is deductible. The IRS calls this technique "income splitting."

6) By hiring a spouse, the owner of a closely held corporation can create an opportunity to take advantage of valuable tax deductions. Sometimes a spouse is not paid a salary because the business sees no advantage to adding another person to the payroll. Then the couple files a joint tax return and half the family income is taxed to each of them, no matter who earns it.

Actually, hiring a spouse for your corporate operations can add some other, equally viable tax-sheltering strategies to your million dollar plan. For example, as an employee, your spouse can participate in such corporate benefits as:

1) Profit sharing—your corporation can get a full deduction for all contributions paid into a legitimate pension and profit-sharing plan for you and your spouse every year. These contributions are not taxable income to your spouse until he or she cashes in on the fund. At that point, these funds will receive a much more favorable tax treatment from the IRS as retirement income.

2) Life insurance—you can purchase life insurance for your employees, including your spouse, and then deduct the cost of the premiums. Any premiums covering the first $50,000 of insurance are not considered income to you or your spouse.

3) Company travel—if your spouse is an employee it is easier to show a legitimate purpose for travel in the employment of the company. While it is often difficult to deduct travel expenses incurred by your spouse, if they are on business trips or conventions, their expenses most likely are deductible.

In some situations, it may even be worthwhile to consider hiring your children for a corporate position and paying them a reasonable wage for the work they perform. Beyond the tax-sheltered benefits we have already outlined, employed children can use the full standard deduction to shield their income from

taxes on the first $3,900 of earned income.

Your company can pay the children money that might otherwise be paid to you or your spouse in salary or dividends at a higher tax bracket and thus shift it into your children's lower bracket. The tax on children's wages starts in the 15% range and stays there for a wide range of incomes.

Everything has to be done completely on the "up and up" when your children work for you. If their wages are not reasonable, or no work is actually performed, the IRS may determine that the children owe back taxes on their earnings and the corporation could lose its deduction.

Remember, no matter how much your children are paid, you still get to claim them as dependents on your income tax return. However, the children cannot claim a personal exemption on their *own* returns if they are claimed as dependents by you.

The IRS rules say that a child is still your dependent as long as you provide more than half of their support and they either:

a) have not reached the age of 19 or
b) are between 18 and 24 *and* are full time students during any five calendar months of the year.

The only way to lose this deduction is if your children spend enough on their own support that at least half of it becomes self-provided. To avoid this problem, have your children put at least half of their earnings into a savings account so that you can always meet the criteria for providing at least half their

support.

The only big drawback to this strategy (besides potentially having to fire your own kids) is that Social Security, unemployment taxes, and other state taxes still have to be paid for all employees, regardless of their age. These taxes can eat up a significant percentage of the tax savings you would gain by hiring them in the first place. Even this is not a major problem if they actually do fill the jobs that would otherwise go to another person, upon whom you would have such taxes anyway.

As long as we are talking about children, let's look at a very interesting strategy for providing them with a hefty little college fund, all tax free through your corporation. Here's how it might work.

Let's say you are using a traditional investment plan to sock away $10,000 of taxable income every year for your children's college savings account. Your children are under 14 years of age, so the taxes on this money would look something like this: After the $500 standard deduction, the next $500 would be taxed at 15% ($75) and the rest at YOUR personal tax rate, say, 33% (another $2,970). That's a total tax bite of $3,045.

Now, if you hire your children and pay them $10,000 over the course of a year for odd jobs at the company, they are only going to pay a little over a $1,000 in taxes on the remainder of their earned income after the standard deduction. The tax savings for you, then, for every year you do this, would amount to over $2,000. By the time they are nineteen, you will have saved $10,000 for their college tuition, all of it tax free.

If you are an owner of a Personal Service Corporation (PSC) you should also take the opportunity to put another worker on the payroll because PSC's pay the flat tax rate of 34%. The more compensation your corporation pays out to family members, the less of its income can be taxed at that astronomical rate.

To avoid any unnecessary IRS scrutiny, you have to be somewhat careful the way you hand out bonuses in your corporation. The criteria for "disguised dividends" can easily be applied to a bonus paid out to yourself or a family member, particularly if there is no obvious reason to warrant such a bonus. If, for example, you were to win a Nobel prize for something you discovered in your work, that would be fairly good grounds for paying yourself a bonus.

Bonuses, then, must be considered a part of your compensation program, especially when it comes to passing that "Reasonableness Test" we've talked about. Most courts have held that a sole shareholder has no right to pay himself a bonus as an incentive to do his best in managing his own company. That is more or less expected of a reasonable person.

Support any bonus program with established criteria, and you will circumvent many problems in this area. Normally, you can give yourself a bonus without attracting IRS attention, provided you tie the bonus to some established, logical, and especially targeted events. As with salary increases, bonuses awarded late in the year are often suspicious. But, if the criteria for payment of a bonus are established earlier in the year, and are based on sensible results like sales quotas or long term company improvements, you shouldn't have any trouble.

You already know that there is an important distinction between capitalizing a

corporation with equity and with debt. A debt holder has no opportunity for growth through the money lent to a corporation, but is in a more secure position than shareholders when it comes to getting that initial investment back. A debt holder gets paid back the money loaned the corporation before any shareholders receive a return of their capital.

In closely held corporations, particularly, debt holders are often shareholders who lend money to their corporation over and above whatever their initial capital investment consisted of. There can be some really favorable tax consequences for a shareholder to do this because while dividends are not tax deductible, interest payments *are* deductible, with some limitations.

There should be a board resolution authorizing the corporation to borrow money from a shareholder and a promissory note issued evidencing the debt. The note should include a fair market interest rate on the loan, as well as all of the terms of payment. Those terms must be followed closely in order to avoid more IRS scrutiny.

For example, let's say your corporation had been capitalized with $100,000 of paid in capital. If the corporation reports a gross income of $70,000 and deductible expenses of $55,000, the $15,000 excess income is then taxable. Any distribution of the profits to the shareholders will result in the double "whammy" of a second tax on their proceeds. But let's suppose, instead of capitalizing the corporation with $100,000, you and your shareholders decided to invest $25,000 in capital stock and provide a loan of $75,000 at 12% interest. What happens to the tax picture then?

Your corporation still shows a gross income of $70,000, but now, deductible

expenses have gone up because of the interest on the note. With $9,000 in deductible interest, total expenses now are $64,000. Taxable income has dropped to $6,000 in this scenario instead of the $15,000 you would have had to report before. And, you and your shareholders still receive as much money (or more) than if the original profits had been distributed through dividends.

The difference is, the loan interest is deductible and no longer subject to double taxation. Unfortunately, the IRS again has discretion in allowing such loan strategies to work. They can declare some or all of the deductions associated with this kind of debt as "constructive dividends" and make you pay additional tax (or penalties) accordingly.

When you lend money to your own corporation, the IRS will be most interested in looking at the ratio of debt to equity that would be reasonable under the existing circumstances of your corporation. This is often referred to as a "thin incorporation" determination. They will be looking closely to see if the debt you've incurred is actually just another form of equity, which makes the interest payments camouflaged dividends.

In situations like this, the IRS will determine loans by a shareholder to be valid, if:

1) A formal written loan document exists that states the details of the loan, including the due date, unconditional promise to pay, terms and interest rate.

2) The corporation has established a valid reason for making the

loan and has board minutes to back it up.

3) There is a limit to the loan, and it does not provide unlimited access to corporate funding.

4) The debt is subordinated to other indebtedness of the corporation, and does not have preference.

5) The ratio of the corporation's debt to equity is within established IRS criteria.

6) The debt is convertible into stock.

Another popular strategy for taking cash out of a corporation is by using leasing. Shareholders who have assets that can legitimately be leased to their corporation enjoy a whole range of options to make money this way. Shareholders can use a partnership or another corporation as the primary leasing company, thereby partially shielding themselves from IRS scrutiny. If a shareholder as an individual, leases buildings, vehicles, equipment, or whatever to the company, tax liabilities and a host of other problems will often result.

There are really three general categories of things that can be effectively leased this way. They are:

1) Employees;
2) Buildings or Real Estate; and
3) Equipment.

Employee leasing is one of the fastest growing trends in corporate business practices. Every big city has companies devoted solely to temporary employees. These companies are generally responsible for all of the human resource management problems inherent with employees, instead of their client companies. They handle interviewing, testing, training, hiring, firing, payroll (including payroll taxes), equal opportunity problems and benefits. Leasing companies charge a fee for all these services, but it is usually based on the total payroll for which they are responsible. On a per-employee basis, it can work out to be a real bargain for some companies.

To take advantage of this opportunity, your primary corporate entity would agree to lease all of its employees from another company, at a cost that is slightly higher than the original payroll, but is still fully deductible. The leasing corporation (your other corporation, ideally) then deducts the total salaries of the employees, along with training costs and other miscellaneous deductions. The end result is that you should be able to take a little more than twice the deduction for salaries than you had the other way, and, you gain a lot more flexibility in your human resource management area.

Okay, what about leasing buildings or real estate? A 1981 Tax Court decision established a method whereby an owner can set up a special tax shelter opportunity by tying the lease of a commercial property directly to the gross sales of the company. This kind of percentage lease has become very popular in commercial real estate ever since. Here's how that original situation came about.

When a food distribution company couldn't find financing for a badly needed warehouse, the corporation's shareholders, a married couple, bought land

and built a warehouse to lease back to their company for 20 years. The company paid all of the property taxes and maintenance costs during that term.

According to the lease, the company was to pay to the couple an annual rent of $60,000, plus 1% of the company's annual gross sales over $4 million. At the time, the company's gross sales were only $2.3 million, so the couple drew the minimum $60,000 rent. Within eight years, the company's sales reached nearly $10 million and the couple received a total rent payment of $118,000.

The IRS attempted to disallow the company's rent deduction over the fixed amount on the basis that it represented a disguised dividend to the shareholders. However, the Tax Court disagreed, ruling that the couple had a legitimate business purpose in entering into the lease agreement, and were entitled to use the same technique with their own company as they would with any other business tenant. When the lease was drawn up, the court said the provisions were fair, thus the lease arrangement was upheld.

In order for you to use this strategy with no "hitches" you must keep all transactions at arm's length, then prove you have a legitimate business purpose, and make sure the terms are reasonable. Getting a certified real estate appraiser to help you with an estimate of fair rental value for the property is always a good idea, too.

Equipment leasing is another way to put money back into your pocket that the IRS wants to take away. Almost any equipment your corporation needs can be leased from somebody, and some of it probably already is. That some-

body might as well be you, or another corporation set up for that purpose.

To accomplish this, capitalize an S corporation to purchase the equipment, then lease it back to your main corporate operations. The monthly lease payments are deducible to the main operation, and their original cost and depreciation are deductible to your S corporation, which should offset any profits. By using the S corporation, you eliminate the double-taxation problem associated with other forms of taking money out of a corporation.

Most owners of small, closely held corporations believe that they have no choice but to live with the heavy burden of "self employment" taxes. Many such owners don't even realize the magnitude of their obligations until it is too late to effectively deal with the problem. However, consulting with a qualified expert to help you set up your corporation before you file can go a long way toward eliminating any big tax surprises.

That's because corporate law provides for some terrific solutions to help people reduce their taxes. For example, one of the simplest strategies is to have an S corporation pay you a salary comparable to the average salary of someone in the work force holding a position similar to yours. The salary you set for yourself should be the lowest amount that you can defend as reasonable to the IRS. Keep in mind that any salary you earn will, of course, be subject to the usual FICA and Medicare taxes.

Once your corporation deducts all its corporate expenses, it can then pay out the remaining net earnings as dividends. Those go to you, as a shareholder. And those dividends will *not* be subject to FICA or Medicare, which helps eliminate at least part of the self-employment tax trap.

When you operate as a C corporation, any losses you suffer when you sell your stock are usually treated as capital losses. They are deductible only against capital gains and up to $3,000 a year in ordinary income. However, if you would like an ordinary loss deduction for your corporate stock, the solution is to treat your stock as "Section 1244 stock."

This means that such stock must have been issued to you by the corporation in exchange for cash but not in exchange for stock or securities in order to qualify for Section 1244 treatment. Also, your corporation must have received more than half of its gross receipts from sources other than rents, royalties, interest, dividends, annuities, and sales or exchanges of securities during the five most recent tax years. And, the corporation cannot have received more than $1,000,000 as a contribution to capital or paid in surplus.

This deduction can be taken for any class of stock, including nonvoting, restricted, and preferred shares. Losses in excess of the $50,000 individual limit ($100,000 on joint returns) are treated as capital losses. Thus, there are no major disadvantages or down sides to using 1244 stock treatment.

IRS Code Section 351 allows shareholders that contribute non-cash assets for their shares to make the transfer without any effect on capital gains or loss. The tax basis of the assets becomes the tax basis of the shares. This type of treatment is only available if the contribution results in the shareholder owning at least 80 percent of the control of the corporation. This can prove to be a highly effective tax strategy.

One of the best tax strategies available now is the incentive for you to invest in small corporations. Individuals who purchase "small business stock" issued after August 10, 1993, and hold the shares for at least five years can escape

tax on *half* their profit when they sell their shares later. The effect of this tax break has been almost unbelievable. Since long-term capital gains have a tax rate cap of 28%, small business stock that qualifies for this break is actually taxed at the effective rate of only 14%.

Small business stock that qualifies for this treatment is referred to as "1202 stock" after the section in the IRC that describes its use. And even more important, that same part of the code says that shareholders who can take advantage of this kind of tax break can be C corporations, S corporations, individuals, partnerships, limited liability companies or mutual funds.

All right, now that we have all of your assets protected, your estate is up and running, including all kinds of protection and benefits, and your corporation is booming, what else could you ask for? How about a little tax free cash?

Before the Tax Reform Act was passed, many companies provided interest free (and tax- free) demand loans to their key executives as fringe benefits. Corporate executives who received interest free loans from their companies were treated as having received "phantom" taxable compensation equal to the value of what the company would have charged on the loan. Executives could then deduct the "phantom" interest expense for the same amount. The end result was that the extra compensation and the deduction canceled each other out and executives paid no tax on the interest free loans.

The Tax Reform Act changed all that. Now, such deductions are subject to rules that eliminate many of the possibilities for tax-free loans. The no tax benefit can still be achieved using some creative strategies on interest free loans. But you must be careful how the loans are structured.

For example, let's look at a $100,000 loan from your corporation at no inter-est. The IRS assumes an interest rate equal to the Applicable Federal Rate (AFR) for low or no-interest loans over $10,000. This is a rate based on the average market yield on U.S. obligations. If the AFR is 7% and you borrow $100,000 at no interest from your company, the *imputed* interest is $7,000. The IRS declares this as additional income to you and taxes it accordingly. You can't avoid the AFR by just charging yourself a token, low interest rate, either. The IRS will again impute as additional income the difference between the rate your corporation charges you and the AFR.

However, interest on a home mortgage can still be deducted, so what if the corporation was to give you an interest free loan secured by your home? The "phantom compensation" and "phantom interest" could be a wash for IRS purposes. You can also borrow from your corporation up to the $10,000 limit, tax free, without paying interest or worrying about taxes. This is the one exception to the taxing rules and should be used sparingly.

Any loan your corporation allows over the $10,000 limit must be structured "at arm's length" to keep the IRS from declaring the loan a taxable corporate dividend. To prove that a loan is an actual transaction that must be repaid, make certain you put all the terms of the deal in writing, including a regular repayment schedule. Also, be sure you record the date and amount of the loan on the corporation's books. The corporate minutes should also reflect full compliance with the loan, including a vote, if necessary, for approval.

Another way to reduce taxes on your corporation is to take full advantage of all Federal tax deductions that allow you to donate excess or inactive inven-tory to schools or charities. Regular C corporations can deduct the *cost* of

the inventory donated, *plus* half the difference between the cost and fair market value. The total deduction can be up to twice the original cost of the inventory.

Most schools will be more than happy to accept outdated equipment, business forms, or miscellaneous office supplies for use in the classroom. However, any donations over $250.00 should be supported by a written acknowledgment. And be *sure* you check out a charity before making any major contributions. Find out if the charity is on the IRS list of organizations approved to receive tax-deductible contributions. You don't want to give away inventory, and then find out the contribution has been disallowed.

> *One of the best ways to reduce your tax bill is by learning what types of expenses are deductible.*

One of the best ways to reduce your tax bill is by learning what types of expenses are deductible. While I have included many of the items which may be deductible to your business, this is by no means an all-inclusive list. Build your relationships with tax professionals, attorneys, and other small business owners so that you can continually learn how to get better deductions all the time.

How can I learn more about and establish a corporation?

Learning about the inner workings of corporations is an absolute must to becoming a Secret Millionaire. The corporation is such an integral part of the overall process that you simply cannot leave yourself without the knowledge of how corporations can and do work for providing asset protection, estate

planning, and tax reduction. Profit Publishing Group, Inc. has developed books, audio and video tapes, software, and educational seminars designed to help you gain the necessary understanding of the area of corporations. Not only that, they also establish corporations and many other entities as well. If you are ready to take control of your finances, call toll-free at 877.868.9742. Call today!

"Dig a well before you are thirsty."
Chinese Proverb

Chapter VI
Secret Millionaire Tool #2:
Limited Partnerships

O ne of the best pieces of advice I've ever heard comes from an old ancient proverb. It is listed at the beginning of this chapter and ties in perfectly with implementing our asset security system. When it comes to preparing yourself for the financial pitfalls that people are so often faced with, it is crucial to understand that the time to plan is before it's too late not after. One of the greatest ways to exercise the principles of the Secret Millionaire is to properly prepare for danger by establishing legal entities. One entity which must be a part of your plan is the limited partnership.

What is a limited partnership?

To fully define the limited partnership, we must first understand the basic concepts which provide the key benefits of the entity, those being limited liability and the partnership form of taxation. Let's take a look at the first concept, limited liability. The partnership form of taxation will be discussed later in the chapter.

Limited liability is a legal term which means that an individual is liable only for the amount of his or her investment in the business. What this means is that personal assets are not available to settle claims against the business in the event of a lawsuit or other action initiated by a creditor. To start with, a *partnership* is an association of two or more persons who join together to carry on a trade or business and share in its profits and losses. A *limited partnership* occurs when one or more of the partners in this association operate in a limited capacity.

To understand the term "limited capacity", we must break it down and analyze it. This limited capacity essentially has two main components:

1. Liability of the limited partner is limited to his or her investment in the trade or business.
2. The limited partner cannot participate in the management or control of the partnership.

The limited partnership is made up of two key types of players. One type is what is known as the general partner, the other is the limited partner. A limited partnership must have at least one general partner. This general partner is personally liable for all debts and obligations of the partnership. The limited partner on the other hand, has only limited liability up to the amount of their investment in the partnership. I bet that makes you want to run right out and become the general partner in a multi-million dollar partnership, doesn't it?

The best way to illustrate the difference between a general partnership and a limited partnership is to take a look at an example. Let's say that three friends decide they'd like to start a business together and they decide that they will all be equal partners in the business. Abe, Bob, and Cecil are general partners of ABC Partnership. ABC Partnership has operating debts of $50,000. Additionally, Abe has secured a $10,000 loan in the partnership name without the other two partners' consent. The net worth of the three general partners is as

follows:

Abe	-$30,000
Bob	$15,000
Cecil	$175,000

ABC Partnership decides to shut its doors. All of a sudden, the creditors come calling. At this point, we must determine who is liable for what? The breakdown would be as follows:

Abe: Abe is personally liable for $60,000. However, his negative net worth does not make him very attractive to creditors. After all, we've all heard the expression, "You can't squeeze blood from a turnip." Abe is essentially judgment-proof and probably not overly concerned about the negative business repercussions.

Bob: Since he is a general partner, Bob is personally liable for $60,000, even the $10,000 that Abe entered into without his knowledge. Bob's net worth is not enough to satisfy to debts, but it is still available to creditors.

Cecil: Cecil is also personally liable for the entire $60,000 of debt. His personal financial statement makes him a very attractive target to creditors. He will probably end up paying the $60,000 personally. The good

news is that he can sue Abe and Bob for their share of the debt. The bad news of course, is that they don't have anything. Notwithstanding this fact, Cecil will be encouraged by numerous attorneys to file suit against Abe and Bob in order to obtain a judgment that he may someday collect on. Good luck.

Friendship: While Abe, Bob, and Cecil were good enough friends to decide to go into business together, it is highly unlikely that they will remain so. One of the worst parts of a general partnership situation is the ill feeling that result upon the dissolution of the partnership. This is especially damaging when money is owed on another's behalf.

Now let's take a look at how a lot of this could be avoided. Let's assume that ABC Partnership was ABC Limited Partnership with Abe and Bob as general partners, and Cecil as the limited partner. Essentially, Abe and Bob come to Cecil with an idea for starting a business. Cecil is not interested in taking an active role in the business but is always interested in new ways to make money. As such, Cecil tells Abe and Bob that he will invest some money in the venture but is not interested in exposing himself to any liability. In this case, the end result with regard to Abe and Bob has not changed, except that Bob will probably get hit for what little he has. Cecil, however, is not personally liable for any of the debts. He can chalk this up to a bad business venture and look for other opportunities to invest his net worth.

This illustrates a key benefit which is offered by forming a limited partnership

rather than a general partnership. However, there a many, many more benefits offered by the limited partnership as we will see in this next section.

What are the advantages of limited partnerships?

Limited partnerships have long been a much-used tool when it comes to asset protection, estate planning, and tax reduction. Let's take a look at some of the advantages of limited partnerships over other forms of business entities.

- **Low start-up costs**- The costs of forming a corporation or LLC can be significantly more than those of forming a partnership. The reason for this is not so much that it costs less to draft the documents but that there is less formality associated with limited partnerships. The initial drafting will cost essentially the same but the follow-up work is significantly less.

- **Low annual filing fees**- Corporations and LLCs are usually subject to some type of franchise or similar tax in the states they do business in. Generally, partnership fees are much lower, if they exist at all.

- **Flexibility in management**- As compared to a corporation, a limited partnership is easier to operate and less structured than a corporation. In a corporation, shareholders own the company, the board of directors manage the company, and the officers oversee the day to day operations of the company. Even if the same person or persons operate in all three capacities, corporate records must still be reported in a way that shows how the three groups work together. In a limited partnership, there is no layered tier of control. The only rule is that the limited partner(s) cannot

participate in the company's management.

- **Pass-through taxation-** Partnerships themselves do not pay taxes. Partnership income and loss is passed through to the individual partners. Corporation profits are often subject to double taxation, once at the corporate level and again at the personal level. This pass-through taxation feature enables the partnership form of doing business to avoid double taxation.

- **Ownership interest protected-** Ownership interests in the limited partnership are usually protected from personal creditors, as opposed to corporate stock, which can be extremely vulnerable if not properly structured.

- **No restrictions on who can be a partner-** S Corporations put restrictions on who can and cannot be a shareholder. Partnerships have no such restrictions. This allows for structuring which can downplay if not eliminate disadvantages.

- **Limited partners are not liable for partnership debts-** As illustrated in the example with ABC Limited Partnership, limited partners (unlike general partners) are not personally liable for debts incurred on behalf of the partnership.

- **Availability of additional sources of capital-** Since limited partners exercise no control over the partnership, additional limited partners can be added without diluting control.

What are the disadvantages of limited partnerships?

There are two main disadvantages that come to mind when dealing with limited partnerships. They are:

1. Every limited partnership must have at least one general partner who is personally liable for the debts of the partnership.
2. Limited partners have no control over the management of the partnership.

> *...part of being a Secret Millionaire is that you adopt a different mindset from the average person. Secret Millionaires view disadvantages as challenges.*

Now, let's start to have some fun with this. Remember, part of being a Secret Millionaire is that you adopt a different mindset from the average person. Secret Millionaires view disadvantages as challenges. We must learn strategies to turn these two potential disadvantages into tremendous advantages.

Problem #1: Liability of general partner

There is no way we can get around the unlimited liability of the general partner, so let's not focus on the liability aspect. Let's focus on the general partner. From our discussion earlier, we learned that one advantage of a partnership was that there were no restrictions on who could be a partner. After reading chapter five of this book, what did you learn about corporations? Remember, corporations themselves have limited liability. Since we know that there are no restrictions on who can become a partner, what would happen if we made

the general partner a corporation?

This corporation would now be subject to all claims of creditors of the partnership. But guess what, the corporation has limited liability. Only the assets of the corporation would be subject to the creditor's claims. Guess who controls what assets are in the corporation? That's right, the corporate board of directors. Who appoints the corporate board of directors? The shareholders of the corporation do. Who do you think would be the ideal shareholders of the corporation? You, of course.

What this scenario has done is virtually eliminate the possibility that a creditor of the partnership can attack any individual personally for his or her claims against the partnership.

Problem #2: Control of the limited partnership

You probably already know the answer to this one. Who controls the limited partnership? The general partner, right? You see, the same ownership structure we used to solve problem #1 essentially solves problem #2.

The key to effectively dealing with any problem is to obtain the knowledge to counteract perceived and potential disadvantages. This is not necessarily the type of mentality that you will encounter when speaking with many professionals. Too often, professionals will focus on the negatives and not enough on the positives. For instance, I have heard many professionals tell clients that a limited partnership is not a good business tool. Well, to be perfectly honest with you, I agree. Let me clarify that. I agree that a limited partnership is not the best tool to have if you are looking for one entity that will solve all your

problems, cure all your ills, take care of all potential pitfalls. But as I pointed out earlier in the book, such an entity simply does not exist.

The key is to have a plan; not just a single entity. When designing an overall asset security system, you better believe that a limited partnership is a crucial ingredient to your success. For one, it is a tremendous source of asset protection as you will see in this next section.

How does a limited partnership help me with asset protection?

Let me take this time to re-emphasize the three main components of The Secret Millionaire philosophy:

1. Asset Protection
2. Estate Planning
3. Tax Reduction

In this section, we will look at some of the key areas of asset protection that a limited partnership provides. Utilizing a corporation as a general partner, as described in the preceding section, helps to minimize the risk of loss associated with the general partner. We will now turn our attention to asset protection as it pertains to the limited partner.

First, let's make sure we all understand just exactly what we mean by claims against a limited partner. Remember, a limited partner has limited liability when it comes to obligations of the partnership. A limited partner can only

lose his or her investment in the business. Therefore, a limited partner already has asset protection against claims arising from business. What we are talking about here are personal claims. These are claims against the limited partner that happen outside the activity of the partnership.

I've spoken many times to many people on the numerous ways and the likelihood of you facing a lawsuit during your lifetime. If we all agree that this is a very likely and probable occurrence, we must now formulate exactly how my capacity as a limited partner can help me protect my assets?

Once again, let's put names and dollars amounts in our discussion to help bring the point home. Let's assume that Huey, Dewey, and Louie joined together to form Ducks Family Limited Partnership. Huey and Louie are the general partners and Dewey is the limited partner. Dewey contributed $100,000 three years ago and received a 50% interest in the business. Over the last three years Ducks Family Limited Partnership has an average income of $300,000 per year. Huey and Louie, acting in their management capacity, decided to distribute the profits of the FLP based on the 50-25-25 ownership ratios in each of the preceding years.

Driving home from his Uncle Donald's house, Dewey rear-ended the vehicle of a Mr. G. Reed. G. Reed immediately began to complain of back and neck pain, along with soft tissue damage, and within days filed suit against Dewey for $10,000,000. Dewey, not having adequate legal counsel, loses the suit and G. Reed is awarded $1,000,000 in damages. Insurance companies pay G. Reed $250,000. Dewey is able to pay G. Reed $150,000. All Dewey is left with is his homestead and his family limited partnership interest. G. Reed wants more.

THE SECRET
MILLIONAIRE

Let's begin by analyzing what Dewy has at risk.

1. 50% ownership interest in Ducks Family Limited Partnership

2. Future profits and distribution from Ducks Family Limited Partnership

The main asset protection feature of the limited partnership is that a creditor of one of the partners, whether a general partner or limited partner, cannot seize his or her limited partnership interest. In other words, G. Reed does not now own 50% of Ducks Family Limited Partnership.

> *The main asset protection feature of the partnership is that a creditor of one of the partners,...cannot seize...partnership interest.*

This really ticks G. Reed off, so he goes back to court and gets a charging order against Dewey's limited partnership interest. The charging order gives G. Reed the right to claim any profits or proceeds payable to Dewey. This order still does not make G. Reed a partner. He only now has rights to the income.

Dewey now feels defeated. He now owns 50% of the FLP, but he cannot share in the profits until his judgment is paid off. Huey and Louie, having attended my seminars in the past, are tickled to death with this situation. Let's go back and re-emphasize two very important characteristics of limited partnerships.

1. The general partner(s) manage the day to day operations of the

partnership. The limited partner has no management control.

2.   For tax purposes, limited partnerships are a pass-through entity. Income and loss are taxed at the personal level.

In year four, Ducks Family Limited Partnership once again has a net income of $300,000. Huey and Louie decide that a distribution of profits is not in the best interest of the partnership this year. They, in their management capacity, decide to reinvest the profits into the business in order to expand operations. G. Reed is furious. He goes back to court to attempt to have the court order Huey and Louie to distribute his 50% of the profits ($150,000). G. Reed loses because he only has the rights which Dewey had; i.e., limited rights and no control over management decisions.

Next, Huey and Louie engage yours truly to prepare their partnership income tax return for the current year. K-1s (a term which we will explain later) showing the individual partner's allocation of income are sent as follows:

Huey	$75,000
Louie	$75,000
G. Reed	$150,000

That's right. G. Reed has inherited the right to pay tax on $150,000. Since G. Reed received no money from the partnership, he will have to pay the taxes from his other personal sources. Not so surprisingly, G. Reed now seems eager to settle this suit for much less than the judgment he won.

In reality, attorneys virtually never attempt to go after a limited partnership because of the asset protection features they carry with them. These features

have some teeth in them that make them a tremendous planning tool. Structured properly, perhaps Dewey could have transferred more of his personal net worth into the limited partnership and actually paid G. Reed less.

How does a limited partnership help me with estate planning?

Estate taxes, as discussed in Chapter 3, are the most severe taxes the IRS levies on an individual. Estate taxes are one of the most detailed and technical areas of the U.S. Tax Code. Failure to plan your estate for your eventual death has cost many, many Americans hundreds of thousands of dollars each.

Warning: *Do not try this at home!*

As I said earlier, estate taxes are extremely brutal. Mistakes can cost tens, even hundreds of thousands of dollars. In this section, we will talk about some estate planning techniques with regard to limited partnerships. I want to emphasize that these strategies should only be implemented by a competent advisor. Now, if that didn't scare you, maybe this will:

> Lowest Estate Tax Rate 18% (only on the first $10,000)
> Highest Estate Tax Rate 60%

And now the good news: You will not have to pay a dime of estate taxes on your estate, I promise. I'm not saying your children won't, but I guarantee that *you* won't.

With a fairly decent understanding of a limited partnership, let's try to tackle

estate planning. A basic form of estate planning is the gifting of assets during one's lifetime. An individual can gift up to $10,000 per person per year. That means a husband and wife could gift their son $20,000 and his wife $20,000 (for a total of $40,000 each year) without having to pay gift taxes. This could add up rather quickly, especially if you have multiple children.

With that in mind, let's go to our example.

Mr. and Mrs. Cash are trying to decide what to do with their estate to best benefit their three daughters. Mr. and Mrs. Cash have a taxable estate, after exclusions, of $1,000,000. If they were to die now, estate taxes on this amount would be $345,800. They could begin to gift each year to their children, but they would no longer have control over the assets given. Mr. and Mrs. Cash have decided to form a family limited partnership with their three daughters.

If Mr. and Mrs. Cash contributed the $1,000,000 to the FLP and their daughter's each received a 25% interest, the girls have effectively received a $250,000 gift which would be subject to gift tax. One advantage of a limited partnership is that assets can be gradually gifted to your heirs. Mr. and Mrs. Cash could gift their daughters an interest in the FLP equal to $10,000 per year and not incur any gift taxes. Over time, a significant amount of assets, if not all of them, could be transferred to the girls. As long as Mom and Dad held a 1% general partnership interest, they would continue to remain in control of the assets. When Mr. and Mrs. Cash pass on, the amount of partnership interest that had been gifted to their daughters would not be subject to estate or inheritance taxes.

If Mr. and Mrs. Cash's estate was made up of primarily real property, the

FLP has made it much easier to transfer those assets to your heirs. Instead of dividing the real property in thirds, they could simply transfer one-third ownership in the entity that owns the real property to their children.

Estate planning with the use of a limited partnership can get much more complex. Discounted values, life insurance, and combining FLPs with trusts make this area of knowledge much too complex to address in this book alone. That is why you must seek out competent, professional help when planning your estate. If you are interested in receiving information on some of the more advanced estate planning strategies available with limited partnerships, call Profit Publishing Group, Inc. toll-free at 877.868.9742.

How does a limited partnership help me reduce my taxes?

Tax reduction is always one of my favorite aspects of the Secret Millionaire concept. You see, taxes are a matter of law. The law is the judge. The IRS has its view of the law, and I have mine. It's kind of like a chess match. The game changes every year, as the IRS corrects its mistakes. You must stay on top of your tax reduction goal. Remember, tax liabilities are generated throughout the year. We only seem to give them special attention when it is time to pay them. By then, it is too late.

> *You must stay on top of your tax reduction goal.... tax liabilities are generated throughout the year. We only...give them special attention when it is time to pay them. By then, it is too late.*

I can see two main areas in which a limited partnership can help reduce taxes:

1. Deductions the entity is allowed to write off.
2. Income-shifting

A limited partnership is a business entity. As you learned in the previous chapter on corporations, a business entity is allowed to write off certain expenses and the partners pay taxes on the net income from the business. This is different from you and me. As individuals, we pay taxes on our gross income. The IRS does not give us the benefit of writing off our business expenses against our income. I know they say you can itemize your deductions and write them off, but you first must itemize, reduce the deductions by 2% of your gross income, and give up your first born male child in order to significantly gain a tax break.

Perhaps the most beneficial income tax strategy that a limited partnership has to offer is the concept of income shifting. Remember back in Chapter 4 when we talked about tax planning? We looked at the different rates at which individuals pay income tax. The more you make, the larger percentage you pay. Also remember that limited partnerships are pass-through tax entities. Combining these two concepts, let's look at the following:

Jack and Jill set up a family limited partnership (FLP) with their three children: Bart, Clyde, and Earl. The FLP expects to make income from its assets of $15,000 this year.

Additional personal taxable income information is as follows:

Jack and Jill	$175,000	36% tax bracket
Bart	$40,000	28% tax bracket

| Clyde | $20,000 | 15% tax bracket |
| Earl | $0 | 0% tax bracket |

If Jack and Jill had not set up the FLP, they would have to pay tax on the entire $15,000, resulting in a tax of $5400 ($15,000 x 36%). If each party owned a 25% interest in the FLP, the resulting tax liabilities would be:

Jack and Jill	$1350
Bart	$1050
Clyde	$563
Earl	$0

This setup results in a total tax of $2963, or a tax savings of $2437. The ownership interests can be manipulated to achieve the optimum result between estate planning and tax reduction, but you get the idea.

It is important to note that the IRS does not like limited partnerships set up with no other apparent purpose than to save taxes. If successful, the IRS can have these entities invalidated. The limited partnership must primarily be created to conduct business or invest. This is just another reason you need to surround yourself with trusted, competent people giving you advice.

Limited partnerships can be tremendous opportunities for tax reduction. The implementation of this strategy is just another step you can take to defend yourself against the IRS.

How can I learn more about and implement a limited partnership?

Learning about the inner workings of limited partnerships is an absolute must to becoming a Secret Millionaire. The limited partnership is such an integral part of the overall process that you simply cannot leave yourself without the knowledge of how limited partnerships can and do work for providing asset protection, estate planning, and tax reduction. Profit Publishing Group, Inc. has developed books, audio and video tapes, software, and educational seminars designed to help you gain the necessary understanding of the area of limited partnerships. Not only that, they also establish limited partnerships and many other entities as well. If you are ready to take control of your finances, call toll-free at 877.868.9742. Call today!

*"It is not enough to have a good mind.
The main thing is to use it well."*
ReneDescartes

CHAPTER VII
SECRET MILLIONAIRE TOOL #3:
LIMITED LIABILITY COMPANIES

I'm sure you know someone who is always telling you what you can and can't do due to the fact that they have acquired a vast amount of knowledge and formal education. We've all known those who are quick to tell you that something won't work as well as all the reasons why. Oftentimes, these individuals are to be greatly respected for their knowledge. They may have attended some of the finest institutions in our country, not to mention those in other countries as well. The problem is that these people may have the knowledge but they don't know how to effectively use it.

Some of the smartest people I've met have not even been college educated. That certainly doesn't mean that I think a college education is worthless; quite the opposite. When I set out to gain knowledge I went not only to college but to law school as well. After that I began studying to obtain a Master's Law Degree in Taxation. The point I want to make however is that knowledge is indeed worthless if not properly implemented. When it comes to establishing a security system for protecting your family's hard-earned assets, using the knowledge

> *...knowledge is indeed worthless if not properly implemented.*

becomes of paramount concern. First, however, you must obtain that knowledge. One item you must learn about is the limited liability company. We will begin this chapter by answering the question, "What is a limited liability com-

pany?"

What is a limited liability company?

I don't know about you, but I'm a bit of a history buff. Do you remember back in high school taking American History and reading about The Great Compromise? Back when our forefathers were laying the foundation for our great nation, there was a very heated debate between the large and small states. Large states wanted representation in Congress to be based on population. Small states wanted each state to be represented equally. The resulting compromise is still what exists in our government today. Congress was created with two separate bodies, the Senate and the House of Representatives. The House was a representation of states based on population. The Senate was represented equally by all states.

Now, being the rational person I am, I want to know why this was called The Great Compromise? Shouldn't it have been named The Common Sense Compromise? What was so "great" about it? The answer seems so obvious to you and me. I guess that's why I'm not a politician.

Two hundred and one years after the founding of our great nation, in 1977, the state of Wyoming passed the first legislation of what it referred to as a limited liability company, or LLC, in the United States. Since that time, all fifty states and the District of Columbia have authorized the organization of LLCs in their jurisdiction.

Two hundred and one years from now, business students and entrepreneurs might just be reading about this event as the Great Compromise as it relates to

business. You see, for years attorneys have been on the side of corporations because of the unlimited liability features they provide. Accountants have consistently advised clients that partnerships provided stronger long-term tax advantages than corporations. Americans were left to choose what meant the most to them, asset protection or tax reduction. The formation of the limited liability company has combined the limited liability feature of the corporation with the tax advantages of the partnership. As a result, the LLC is the fastest growing business entity in existence today.

LLC Growth:		
	1989	2 states
	1990	4 states
	1991	8 states
	1992	18 states
	1993	36 states
	1996	48 states
	1999	50 states

Let me ask you, how many of you can remember seeing the letters "Inc." at the end of a business name? Everybody has, of course. That is because for years the corporation was the dominant form of conducting business. Now let me ask you, how many of you can remember seeing the letters "LLC" at the end of a business name? I would say most people have noticed this. Now, can anyone remember seeing "LLC" in a business name ten years ago? I would be surprised if anyone could.

You see, limited liability companies are brand new in the United States. Many people are just now realizing the powerful tool they can be. Let's go back to our list. What are the three goals that a Secret Millionaire attempts to achieve?

1. Asset Protection
2. Estate Planning
3. Tax Reduction

The remainder of the chapter deals with the LLC as it relates to the three components above. Since an LLC is a combination of two of my favorite entities, the corporation and the limited partnership, you will definitely notice some similarities if you have attended my seminars or read my books in the past. The LLC was created to take advantage of these similarities so it seems quite obvious that they must be included as part of a discussion on the limited liability company as a tool for the Secret Millionaire. We'll start by taking a look at the advantages and disadvantages of the entity.

What are the advantages of limited liability companies?

Let's look specifically at the advantages of limited liability companies in comparison to corporations and partnerships.

LLC Advantages Over Corporations

- **Pass-through taxation:** Distributions of profit in a corporation are known as dividends. These are taxed once at the corporate level and once again at the individual level, hence the term "double taxation". The same occurrence results when a corporation is liquidated and assets are transferred to the shareholders. Since the LLC has no tax at the LLC level, items of taxation are "passed through" to the members and taxed only once at the individual level.
- **Lack of corporate formalities:** Corporations must be managed by a

board of directors who are elected by the shareholders. Minutes of the board of directors meetings must be kept. An LLC can be managed by its members and there is no requirement to document minutes of meetings, although this might be a good idea.

Another question I get all of the time is, "What about "S" corporations?" An "S" corporation is essentially a pass-through tax status that a traditional corporation can elect. "S" corporations are perhaps the most common form of small business entity around today. So if an "S" corporation has pass-through taxation features, what is the difference between it and an LLC. Let's take a look at some of the specific advantages an LLC has over an "S" corporation.

LLC Advantages Over "S" Corporations

- **An LLC is not limited to one class of stock.** In an "S" corporation, each share of stock must have the same rights as every other share of stock when it comes to corporate profits and corporate assets. For example, if A, B, & C are equal shareholders in a corporation and the "S" corporation decides to distribute it's profits of $15,000, A, B, & C would each receive $5,000. This is fair, but it is not flexible. An LLC is extremely flexible in its profit/loss allocation.
- **Any individual or entity can be a member of an LLC.** An "S" corporation's shareholders are limited to individuals, estates, certain trusts, and other "S" corporations. Shareholders must also be citizens or residents of the United States. Thus, a non-resident alien cannot be a shareholder of an "S" corporation. "C" corporations, partnerships and IRAs cannot be shareholders of an "S" corporation.

- **An LLC is not limited to the number of members it can have.** An "S" corporation is limited to 75 shareholders. For most of the people reading this book, this is not that big of an issue.

- **The tax treatment of a properly formed LLC is automatic.** In contrast, a corporation must timely file a proper "S" election in order to receive preferential tax treatment.

- **The liquidation of an LLC is generally a tax-free event.** A liquidation of an "S" corporation interest is a taxable event as if the corporation sold the liquidated assets to the shareholder at their fair market value. This advantage makes the LLC a particularly ideal entity for holding real estate.

- **An LLC is not required to maintain corporate formalities**. An "S" corporation must still comply with the record keeping and bookkeeping formalities that traditional corporations do.

- **An LLC can possibly help in reducing FICA taxes at the personal level**. An "S" corporation must pay a shareholder a "reasonable wage" for services he or she renders. These wages trigger the dreaded FICA taxes discussed in our section on tax reduction. Currently, only guaranteed payments to members of an LLC are subject to FICA taxes. There is no "reasonable wage" clause. Don't expect this loophole to be around too long, however.

LLC Advantages Over Partnerships

By now you know that an LLC has the tax benefits of a partnership. After reading the previous chapters, we also know that a partnership can be formed as a limited partnership to help limit an individual partner's liability. For our

discussions here, when we mention partnerships we are talking about limited partnerships. What, then, are the advantages of an LLC over a limited partnership?

- **All members of an LLC maintain limited liability.** A limited partnership is required to have at least one general partner who is personally liable for the debts of the partnership. This is not the case with an LLC
- **Members of an LLC can participate in management without losing their limited liability status.** Remember, if a limited partner participates in the management of the partnership, he or she is exposed to personal liability. One can only have limited liability in a limited partnership if there is no control. In the LLC, there is not such requirement.

In our discussion on limited partnerships earlier, we mentioned that one asset protection feature of a limited partnership was to have a corporation become the general partner. The LLC accomplishes this same result without the use of multiple entities. That equates to lower overall paperwork and maintenance costs such as tax returns, accountants' fees, filing fees, franchise taxes, etc.

What are the disadvantages of limited liability companies?

Obviously, the limited liability company does not satisfy all of our concerns. If the LLC was the perfect entity, there would be no need to discuss alternative ways of doing business. Let's analyze some of the key disadvantages of limited liability companies.

- **LLCs do not have a large body of case law.** Corporations have been around for years. Corporations have sued and been sued for just about everything under the sun. The IRS has attacked and re-attacked every area of corporate tax law. As a result, just about any stance you wish to take with corporations with regards to asset protection, estate planning, and tax reduction is well-documented with specific case history. LLCs do not have this luxury. They have still yet to experience all of their growing pains.

- **LLC members in high personal brackets could face higher taxes.** The characteristic of pass-through taxation places the burden of tax on the individual member. Income from LLCs is taxed directly to members based on their membership interests, regardless of whether or not the member actually takes the income out of the business. Thus, an individual who wishes to leave profits in the business and not take a distribution could pay lower marginal tax rates as a corporation as opposed to LLCs. This disadvantage can be easily overcome by adequate planning.

- **Initial filing fees for LLCs can be more expensive in some states.** Some states require that an LLC publish a notice in specified legal journals or other papers. This cost can be as much as $1000 or more. Corporations are not required to do this in all states.

- **An LLC must generally use a calendar year.** A corporation has greater flexibility to use a fiscal year. A fiscal year is a tax year that ends at the end of any month other than December. This corporate advantage can create situations where individuals can basically defer paying income taxes for a year while achieving a current corporate tax deduction.

- **LLCs do not have continuity of life.** Corporations continue to exist regardless of events that happen to its shareholders personally. By law, an LLC dissolves upon death, dissolution, bankruptcy, or after a specified

period of time (i.e. 50 years), depending on state law. This period of time, however, can usually be extended.

- **The transferability of interests in an LLC is limited.** Therefore, it would not be a favorable entity for a large business looking to go public and retain partnership taxation.

- **Conversion of an existing business to LLC status will probably result in a taxable transaction.**

As you can tell, there are some fine lines between the different types of entities and how they can be used. I would not listen to anyone who says you should be this or that entity without looking at the circumstances. The bottom line is that LLCs are here to stay, so ignoring them would not be a wise financial decision.

How does a limited liability company provide asset protection?

Asset protection with a limited liability company is very similar to that of a limited partnership. There is one major difference, however, which we talked about earlier. In an LLC, all members have limited liability, or limited partner status. In a limited partnership, remember, there must be at least one general partner who is liable for all debts of the partnership.

Over the last few years, my seminars, videos, tapes, and books have not covered the subject of the LLC and asset protection. This is because LLCs were so new. Nobody had figured out how they worked. During my seminars in that period, the audiences I spoke to enjoyed no other discussion more in the asset protection area than the section that deals with the limited partner-

ship and the charging order. I had people wanting to form an LP just for the opportunity to use the charging orders against potential creditors.

Well guess what? I have good news for those of you interested in the charging order. The same charging order strategy that applies to limited partnerships also applies to limited liabilities companies. In case you have forgotten or have never been exposed to how a charging order works, let's go through the following example.

Myles, Theodore, and Bubba are the only three members of Bubba's Burgers, LLC. Each has a one-third interest. Bubba's Burgers, LLC is one of the fastest growing food chains in the South, reporting net income of $100,000 in each of it's first two years. After receiving financial statements for the third year of operations, Bubba goes to the local bar to celebrate their income of $250,000 for year three. After several cool ones, Bubba and Norm begin a debate on who was the better football team, the 1985 Chicago Bears or any Dallas Cowboy team to ever take the field. Tired of listening to the bellyaching of the die-hard silver and blue loyalist, Bubba knocks out three of Norm's front teeth. Norm is immediately sent to the emergency room. Not long after, Bubba is served with a lawsuit for $3,000,000. After a short trial, Norm is awarded a judgment in the amount of $250,000.

Being wiped out by a divorce five years earlier, Bubba can only satisfy $50,000 of the judgment with his personal assets. Norm wants a piece of Bubba's Burgers in order to satisfy his judgment. Norm goes back to court to get a charging order against Bubba's LLC interest.

The charging order gives Norm the right to receive the income distribution

from Bubba's LLC interest. Norm has no voting rights or management powers. After franchising Bubba's Burgers, LLC in the Northeast, the company financial statements show a $600,000 net income for year four. Norm is ecstatic and is ready to receive the rest of his settlement. Myles and Theodore, being astute in the area of asset protection after attending one of my seminars, decide not to distribute any of the LLC profits. Instead, they put the money back for expansion in the Midwest. Norm petitions the court to demand the LLC to release Bubba's share of income. The courts do not listen.

If we remember the LLC and its pass-through form of taxation, Norm now has to pay taxes on the percentage of income allocated to Bubba, even though the money was not distributed. That means Norm has to pay taxes on $200,000 he did not receive. On April 16, after writing a rather large check to the IRS, Norm settles with Bubba for $25,000.

The concept of the charging order has long been a staple in asset protection strategies with regards to limited partnerships. It is now just as powerful a tool with limited liability companies.

> *The concept of the charging order has long been a staple in asset protection strategies with regards to limited partnerships.*

Another example of the valuable asset protection strategy the LLC has to offer comes in the area of real estate investment. LLCs are arguably the best form of business organization for the ownership of real property. This status is achieved because of three main reasons:

1. The pass-through taxation aspect of the LLC eliminates the corporate problem of double taxation on the eventual sale of

the property.

2. No member of an LLC is personally liable for the debts or liabilities of the LLC.

3. LLC members can fully participate in the management of the LLC without jeopardizing their limited liability status.

By now, you probably have these three advantages of an LLC etched in your mind. These are the main reasons the LLC is rapidly becoming so popular. Nowhere do these three components flex their muscle more than in the area of real estate investment. Let's take a look at what I mean.

Dave is on his way to becoming a real estate tycoon. He owns ten major pieces of commercial rental property in his city. Dave was properly advised that a corporation was not the proper business entity to operate his real estate ventures out of because of the double taxation issues. Therefore, Dave set up a limited partnership to run his business.

Grace was on her way into a grocery store that Dave's LP leases. As she was walking on the sidewalk, she slipped on a banana peel and broke her arm. Because of the fact that Grace was a concert pianist, she was forced to miss performances for several months. She even began to suffer traumatic flash-backs to the painful event she had suffered through. Grace successfully sued Dave's LP and won a judgment of $2,000,000 for compensatory damages alone. Dave had planned ahead and had properly set up a corporation as the general partner of the LP. Therefore, the assets of the LP and the assets of the managing corporation are at risk.

Just two weeks later, Dave's LP was sued by Frank. The movie theater that

Dave's LP owned was not equipped with an adequate handicap entrance for Frank's wheel chair. Looking to make a statement, the court slapped Dave's LP with a judgment of $5,000,000.

After insurance paid off, Dave's LP still owed the two parties a total of $5,000,000. Since Dave has only been in business for six years, he still owes substantial mortgages to the bank for each of the ten properties. Dave could attempt to sell all his properties, but he doesn't have enough equity to cover the judgment. Selling the properties would also generate a tax hit Dave could not handle. Dave is faced with the possibility of losing all of his rental properties.

OK, let's substitute an LLC in place of the limited partnership. What have we done to help the situation? The answer is "not much"? Basically, the corporate general partner is off the hook. The assets of the LLC are still at risk.

Now, what if each of the ten rental real estate properties were operated as its own LLC? Each LLC owned the property, collected rents, and paid the mortgages and expenses of the individual property. In our example above, Dave would only be at risk for two of the properties, instead of all ten.

An inherent problem in real estate investing is the enormous potential risks of liability that come into play. Mortgage liability, environmental liability, and public access liability are just a few of the nightmares that property owners have to deal with.

The key to asset protection with the limited liability company, as with any entity, is planning. Asset protection should be done before it is needed. Once

How does a limited liability company provide estate planning?

> *...estate planning is just that, planning. It has to be done over one's lifetime. It cannot be done at the last minute.*

Another area that the limited liability company is helpful with is the field of estate planning. Estate planning is a broad term. I like to think of estate planning as maximizing the amount of assets one has accumulated during their lifetime that will inevitably pass to their heirs. Once again, estate planning is just that, planning. It has to be done over one's lifetime. It cannot be done at the last minute.

Since estate planning entails maximizing your assets, the current advantages LLCs have to offer in asset protection and tax reduction automatically make it a valuable estate planning tool.

One of the biggest problems with estate planning is that people do not know how severe estate taxes can be. Estate taxes can be as high as 50-60% depending on the size of the estate. The lowest estate tax rates are only 18%. That can be quite a chunk of change. Taxpayers get to exclude from their estate the following amounts:

1999	$650,000
2000-2001	$675,000
2002-2003	$700,000
2004	$850,000

| 2005 | $950,000 |
| 2006 | $1,000,000 |

To truly grasp the importance of estate planning, we need to take a look at an example. Let's take a hypothetical client, Sue, who has an estate that consists of the following:

Cash	$100,000
Investments	$200,000
Retirement Plan	$250,000
House	$150,000
Life Insurance	$300,000

Sue dies in the year 2002. Her total estate is $1,000,000. That's right, life insurance is included in the estate. After deducting her estate exemption, Sue's taxable estate is $300,000, resulting in an estate tax of $87,800. Doesn't estate planning seem important now?

As for the estate tax exclusions that reach $1,000,000 by the year 2006, I think the Kiplinger Tax Letter put it best when it said:

"Warning: Future Congresses Have Ample Time to Repeal"

Limited liability companies are very similar to limited partnerships when it comes to estate planning. Some of its advantages are as follows:

• Because income is passed through to LLC members, the tax rates may be

lower than those for trusts, which have the highest marginal tax rate (39.6% at $8350).

- LLCs do not have the restrictions on who can be a member that an "S" corporation does. Thus, an LLC can have a trust or family limited partnership as a member.

- Upon the death of an LLC member, the remaining members may vote to continue the business of the LLC. The member's LLC interest and the assets of the LLC can be stepped up to the fair value if the proper elections are made. This can reduce the gain that the LLC must recognize on the eventual disposition of the assets.

- LLC interests can be gifted to children, thus reducing the size of the estate that can be taxed.

Let's look at the following example.

Hugh G. State owned a vast amount of farmland in Wyoming worth $3,000,000. Hugh and his wife, Marge, have 7 children and 16 grandchildren. They formed an LLC with their children and grandchildren as members to run the farming operation. Over the years, Hugh and Marge annually gifted percentage interests in the partnership to the 23 family relatives. Both Hugh and Marge gifted the maximum of $10,000 each, enabling each family member to receive an additional $20,000 interest each year. When Hugh and Marge passed away, they retained a 10% interest in the LLC. Their gross estate only has to include $300,000 attributable to the farm.

Estate planning is one of the most complex and often overlooked aspects of personal financial planning. Proper estate planning must use a variety of strategies and techniques in order to pass the maximum amount possible to your

heirs. A properly structured LLC can be a valuable tool in achieving that reality.

How does a limited liability company help me reduce my taxes?

Limited liability companies, as with most other business entities, provide an excellent vehicle to help reduce taxes. Some of the tax advantages of LLCs are listed below.

- LLCs are pass- through entities for taxation purposes, meaning the individual members, not the LLC, pays tax on the business income. An LLC with several members has the opportunity to spread the income out to other members that might be in lower tax brackets.
- LLCs give the taxpayer the ability to deduct expenses from gross income before paying tax.
- LLCs give the taxpayer alternative ways to pay income to it's members (interest, royalties, etc.)
- LLCs have the option of setting up certain types of retirement plans, giving the LLC a current tax deduction and the member tax-deferred income.
- LLCs currently contain laws that may help in reducing FICA taxes on income distributions. This is a definite advantage over partnerships and a statutory advantage over "S" corporations. General partnerships pay FICA taxes on all income. "S" corporation shareholders must be paid a "reasonable wage" for services rendered. This is a very vague concept that the IRS can use in its favor.

Here are a few examples of some tax benefits an LLC can provide:

Bertha and her three daughters, Kristi, Krystal, and Kristine have formed an LLC to operate their music group, Mama B and the Ks. Bertha has long been a music superstar and is receiving large amounts of royalties from her previous smash hits. This puts her in the highest (39.6%) individual tax bracket. Kristi, Krystal, and Kristine all finished high school last year. They marvel at the opportunity at being backup singers for their mother, not to mention getting a piece of the pie as well. This is their first experience at making money, so they are all in the lowest (15%) tax bracket.

Together, their first single reaches the top one hundred. The first dollar of income that is allocated to Bertha begins to be taxed at 39.6%. The first dollar of income that is allocated to each of the girls begins to be taxed at 15%. On the first $25,000 of taxable income they receive, Bertha would pay $9900. The three girls would pay $3750. This results in a tax savings of $18,450 to Bertha by shifting some of the income to the three girls rather than taking it all in her own personal name.

After realizing the tremendous career she had created, Bertha wrote a best selling autobiography, *"Bertha: The Life and Times of a Music Queen."* Bertha set up an LLC to write and distribute the book. She is also considering writing a "how to" book on raising triplets while managing a career. Bertha receives income from the LLC in the form of royalties based on her book sales. These royalties are not subject to FICA taxes as is the case with guaranteed payments. In her "how to" book, Bertha wants each of the girls to write a chapter on what being a triplet was like. If the book sells, each of the three girls can also receive royalty income. Remember, FICA taxes can be as

much as 15.3%. This can add up to tremendous amounts of savings.

Noticing that bystanders wince every time one of her daughters hits a high note, Bertha becomes concerned about their musical future. She does not believe they will make it in this tough industry once she is out of the picture. Bertha decides to set up a retirement plan for her and her girls through their LLC. By now, the group's first single is hovering around top ten status and the money is beginning to roll in. This allows Bertha and each of her daughters to put back $20,000 in a self-employed pension. This creates an $80,000 tax deduction for the LLC and gives each of the members $20,000 of tax deferred income. That's right. The deduction is in the current year, and the tax is not paid until the money is taken out at retirement. The income (interest, dividends, capital gains, etc.) generated by the retirement plan is also not taxed until the funds are taken out at retirement. Bertha is very content with the fact that her girls have already started planning for their retirement. She's heard them sing solo enough to know that music will not put food on their table during the years ahead. By utilizing the limited liability company in conjunction with a retirement plan, Bertha has taken necessary steps to take care of her family both now and in the future. You can do the same.

How can I learn more about and establish a limited liability company?

Learning about the inner workings of limited liability companies is an absolute must to becoming a Secret Millionaire. The limited liability company is such an integral part of the overall process that you simply cannot leave yourself without the knowledge of how limited liability companies can and do work for providing asset protection, estate planning, and tax reduction. Profit Publish-

ing Group, Inc. has developed books, audio and video tapes, software, and educational seminars designed to help you gain the necessary understanding of the area of limited liability companies. Not only that, they also establish limited liability companies and many other entities as well. If you are ready to take control of your finances, call toll-free at 877.868.9742. Call today!

"Men build too many walls and not enough bridges."
Sir Isaac Newton

CHAPTER VIII
SECRET MILLIONAIRE TOOL #4: TRUSTS

The subject of this chapter is essentially about a way to build bridges that will enable you to get from one point to another by overcoming obstacles. As the quote at the top of the page implies, most people spend their time dwelling on obstacles rather than on ways to get around these obstacles. If you spend all of your time, effort and energy concentrating on how great the obstacle is, it tends to make the obstacle an even greater hindrance to accomplishing your objectives than when you first began. Secret Millionaires distinguish themselves from the masses by conquering any barriers that stand in the way of their objectives. One of the ways they do this is through the utilization of trusts.

A trust is indeed a key component of any well-thought plan. However, many people fail to implement a trust into their plan as a result of failing to understand what a trust is all about and how it can help them to protect their assets. Let's begin our quest to build bridges by understanding one of the key building materials in the building process, the trust.

WHAT IS A TRUST?

I don't know about you, but when I hear the word "trust" used in the business sense, I'm not always sure exactly what that means. Attorneys, accountants, and financial planners have made this a very ambiguous term. The concept of

a trust brings to mind things such as wealth, death, and beneficiaries. While trusts definitely have connections with these terms, trusts have an unlimited number of uses for people in various stages of life and wealth.

Any discussion about trusts contains terminology specific to trusts. Let's start by defining the key ingredients of trusts.

Definition of Trust Terms

Beneficiary: a person who has the right to receive income from the trust or the trust corpus.

Corpus: the assets that make of the principal of the trust (money, real estate, etc.)

Fiduciary: a trustee, executor, administrator, or other individual who acts in a trustee capacity for another person.

Fiduciary Duty: the responsibility to act solely for the benefit of another without regard for personal interests.

Grantor: the creator of the trust.

Remainderman: the person entitled to received trust property after the trust ends.

Trustee: the person who holds legal title to property and manages trust assets.

These are the basic terms used in a trust relationship. All trusts have these key components. Let's look at the following example.

Harry is retired and has made a nice living for himself in the real estate business. After consulting with his long-time financial planner, Jerry, he decides to

set up a trust for his daughter, Mary, to ensure her a lifetime income. Harry transfers some rental real estate worth $2,000,000 and $500,000 cash into a trust. Harry wants Jerry to hold title to the property and to manage these assets. Mary is to receive the income from these assets for as long as she lives. Upon her death, the assets in the trust will transfer to her son, Barry. Who are the key players in this trust?

Beneficiary: Mary, she has the right to receive the income from the trust.

Corpus: The real estate and the $500,000. These assets make up the principal of the trust.

Grantor: Harry, he is the one who created the trust.

Remainderman: Barry, he is entitle to receive the trust property when the trust ends.

Trustee: Jerry, he holds legal title to the property and manages the trust assets.

In his capacity as trustee, Jerry is the **fiduciary** and has a **fiduciary duty** to act in Mary's best interest.

In essence, a trust is merely a form of ownership. Legal title to property passes from one individual (grantor) to another individual (trustee). The trustee manages the property in the trust for the benefit of the benficiaries.

A trust has long been viewed as an entity reserved solely for the super-wealthy. If you were not fabulously wealthy like the Rockefellers, Kennedys, or Vanderbilts, then there was no need in wasting your time and money on establishing a trust. Nothing could be further from the truth! There are many different types of trusts out there, and there are just as many reasons for using

THE SECRET
MILLIONAIRE

them. There are trusts for asset protection and estate planning, trusts for avoiding the nightmare of expensive will contests and lengthy probate issues, and trusts that help legally reduce estate taxes. There are so many types of trusts out there that you have no excuse not to take advantage of this vital tool.

Think of a simple trust as a contract between two or more people for owner-ship, control, and management of a property or asset. Like entities which have been discussed in previous chapters, a trust is separate and distinct from whomever created it. It is, in effect, an "artificial person" that holds property and performs specific assigned acts in it's own name for the benefit of one or more parties.

> *Trusts, in simple terms, help people plan for the future.*

Trusts, in simple terms, help people plan for the future. This can mean your future, your spouse or children's future, or basically any other situation which involves financial planning. Properly structured, a trust can:

- Manage assets for your family in the event of your death
- Manage assets for your family if you become disabled
- Save income, gift, and estate taxes
- Own insurance policies
- Avoid probate

Trusts provide an almost unlimited capability for holding and transferring property. Any sound financial plan should incorporate the use of trusts.

What are the different types of trusts?

Have you ever been asked a question that just could not be answered in a few words? If you were to ask a doctor what are the different types of organs in the human body it would take weeks to cover each and every one of them. Odds are Doc would start with the main ones, brain, heart, kidneys, etc. That is not saying that the others are not as important. It is just too overwhelming to include every organ unless you are in medical school. That is similar to the question, "What are the different types of trusts?" The exact answer to that question is overwhelming in scope. In this section we will discuss some of the more common and practical trusts used today. That is not saying that the others are not as important. It is just too overwhelming to include every trust unless you are studying to become a financial planner.

Let's first look at the two basic types of trusts: revocable trusts and irrevocable trusts.

Revocable Trusts: This is a trust in which the grantor (person who creates the trust) retains to right to terminate the trust. The grantor can watch the estate plan operate while he or she is still alive and make any needed changes to the trust as he or she sees fit. Since the grantor has sufficient control over the trust, he or she is still considered the owner for tax purposes. Revocable trust assets are included in the grantor's gross estate for estate tax purposes. The transfer of assets into a revocable trust is not subject to gift tax.

Irrevocable Trusts: This is a trust in which the grantor relinquishes all control over the assets of the trust when those assets are transferred into the trust. An irrevocable trust cannot be changed once established, hence the term irre-

vocable. Irrevocable trust assets are not included in the grantor's gross estate for estate tax purposes. The transfer of assets into an irrevocable trust is subject to gift tax.

Each of these types of trusts serve a particular function. All trusts are either one or the other. Irrevocable trusts are mainly used to avoid estate taxes and to protect assets from the claims of creditors. Revocable trusts are generally used to avoid probate or to provide protection if a person should become disabled. These benefits are covered in more detail later in this chapter.

Let's now take a look at four specific kinds of trusts. They are the living trust, charitable remainder trust, irrevocable life insurance trust, and the asset protection trust. These trusts are some of the tools used by some of todays most successful individuals.

Living Trust

A revocable living trust is perhaps one of the most used tools to avoid the burdensome and expensive costs of probate. To fully understand the advantages of a living trust you must first have some degree of knowledge on what probate is and what it means to you.

> *The fact is probate is not a concept. It is a real problem for millions of Americans.*

Probate is another professional, legal term most people do not understand. In fact, most people choose to ignore this concept because it deals with death, which is not a subject most people like to dwell on. The fact is probate is not a concept. It is a real

problem for millions of Americans. Probate is the legal process used to wind up an individual's legal and financial affairs after their death. Assets and liabilities of the estate are identified. Debts are paid. Taxes are filed. Administrative (attorney) fees are paid. The remaining assets, if any, are distributed to the beneficiaries of the estate as provided by a will, or without a will, in accordance with state law.

On the surface, probate sounds like a nice, tidy process, and conceptually it is. However, once a couple of attorneys, a few accountants, and our rapid moving court system get involved, this process becomes a nightmare. It has been estimated that legal costs for probate are in excess of $2 billion per year. Probate costs can easily amount to 10% or more of the total assets in the estate. An average probate period is probably about nine months. By definition, 50% of probated estates are below average, meaning they take longer to close. It is not out of the ordinary for an estate to be in probate for two or more years. Another big problem with probate is that it is a matter of public record. Privacy is not a concern of the probate process. Anyone, your co-worker, your preacher, your next door neighbor, even your ex-wife can find out what assets, property and money, are part of the estate you stand to inherit. This does not exactly define the idea of a "Secret Millionaire."

A living trust is a trust created by a living person. That makes sense. Our first hurdle is now overcome. We can define a living trust. A revocable living trust then is a trust that is created by a living person and that person retains the right to terminate the trust at any time. Remember the key players in a trust we talked about earlier? We never mentioned a rule that says one individual can only play one part. That's because there is no such rule. The same individual can be the grantor and the trustee. That's right. You can transfer assets into a

trust and name yourself as trustee of those assets. Let's look at this a little closer.

Mr. Black and his wife, Violet, have created a comfortable living for themselves. Mr. Black has heard of the costs and administrative headaches of probate and is searching for a way to avoid this problem. Mr. Black's main objective is to look out for the well-being of his wife and daughter, Amber. Mr. Black has been looking into the use of trusts as a tool to avoid probate, but does not like the idea of relinquishing control of his assets. Mr. Black decides to transfer investments worth $80,000, land worth $150,000, and $50,000 cash into a trust. Mr. Black wants himself and his wife, Violet, to receive the income generated by the assets and have the assets transfer to his daughter, Amber, when he and his wife die. Mr. Black names himself as trustee and wishes to maintain the right to terminate the trust at any time. He also wants Violet to be named successor trustee if he dies first.

Mr. Black has established a revocable living trust. Let's go back to high school and dissect this sentence. Trust is a noun. Revocable and living are adjectives that describe the trust. The trust is revocable because Mr. Black maintains the right to terminate the trust at any time. The trust is living because it was created during Mr. Black's lifetime.

What has changed in Mr. Black's life. The answer is nothing. He still controls the assets he set the trust up with. He has, however, taken a major step in avoiding the perils of probate. Remember, a trust is merely a form of ownership. When Mr. Black dies, Violet becomes the trustee. When Violet dies, the property, or corpus, passes directly to Amber, thus avoiding the problems associated with probate. The assets transferred into the trust were worth

$280,000. If our 10% probate costs is accurate, that would mean probate costs of around $28,000. That is before taking into account assets not transferred into the trusts such as a home, vehicles, or even life insurance.

Charitable Remainder Trusts

Charitable remainder trusts are fast becoming a common tool for individuals with large amounts of wealth. A charitable remainder trust, or CRT, serves three main purposes:

1. Benefit a charity of your choice.
2. Receive a current year tax deduction.
3. Provide an income stream for you and your spouse for life.

Individuals with large amounts of wealth often realize that themselves and their children and grandchildren have been sufficiently provided for. A large amount of tax dollars can be saved by setting up a CRT. Here's how it works. You donate property (real estate, stocks, bonds, investments, cash, etc.) to a charity through the use of the CRT. The charity will not receive the full benefit of the donated property until some future time, usually when you and your spouse pass away. You, being the tax savvy person you are, receive a income tax deduction in the year of the donation equal to the fair market value of the transferred property at the time of the donation. Under this format, you and your spouse maintain an income interest in the CRT. This means the income generated by the assets in the trust will be paid to you and your spouse until you die. The amount of your income tax deduction would be reduced by the present value of the income interest retained by you and your spouse. When you and your spouse pass away, the charity would then receive the full ben-

efits (income) generated by the trust assets.

There are two main types of charitable remainder trusts. They are charitable remainder annuity trusts (CRAT) and charitable remainder unitrusts (CRUT). We have now introduced CRTs, CRATs, and CRUTs. This is where attorneys and financial planners make the big bucks. They have begun to play alphabet soup. With the use of so many letters, abbreviations, and acronyms it is easy for the average person to think this information is too deep for them. Let me remind you that we have only begun to play alphabet soup. There are many more that we will not cover in this book. The reality of it is that a CRAT and A CRUT are simply variations of a CRT. Once you understand how a Charitable remainder trust works, CRATs and CRUTs just fall into place.

Charitable Remainder Annuity Trusts

This type of CRT creates a fixed amount or annuity that will be paid to the income beneficiaries of the trust. The amount of return cannot be less that 5% of the gross value of the trust. Let's say you funded a CRAT with $100,000. You could stipulate in the trust agreement that you were to be paid $7500 per year. If the earnings of the trust were not enough to cover the $7500 payment, then the principal, or corpus, of the trust must be used to satisfy the payment. Once a CRAT is established, additional contributions of trust principal cannot be made. This is an irrevocable trust, which means that once it is established, it cannot be terminated.

Charitable Remainder Unitrust

This type of CRT creates a variable amount or annuity that will be paid to the

income beneficiaries of the trust. As with a CRAT, this variable percentage cannot be less than 5% of the value of the trust principal. This amount is re-valued each year. In essence, a CRUT pays the income beneficiaries based on the annual appreciation of trust assets rather than on the actual income the trust earns. If the income earned by the trust is not enough to cover the required payment, trust principal can be used (thus lowering the required payment for the next year) or the trust could stipulate that the shortfall will be made up at a later time. Let's assume you funded a CRUT with a commercial building worth $200,000. This building receives rents of $36,000 per year. You wanted to retain an income interest equal to 5% of the trust assets. Your first year payment would be $10,000. After collecting rents and re-apprais-ing the building, the trust is valued at $250,000 the following year. Your second year payment would be $12,500. If in later years the real estate market collapses and the trust is valued at $150,000. Your payment would be $7500. The CRUT is also an irrevocable trust. Once it is established, it cannot be terminated.

Comprehensive example of Charitable Remainder Trusts

Jack and Diane own real estate worth approximately $500,000. They pur-chased the land several years earlier for $50,000. If they were to sell the land, capital gains taxes would hit them for about $90,000. Jack and Diane have three main concerns.

1. They want to make sure their son, John, is provided for after their death.
2. They would like a current income stream to help with retirement.
3. They feel they have been blessed and would like to give some-

thing back to the community they live in.

If Jack and Diane were to die before they sold the real estate, the land would be grouped with their other assets and be subject to estate taxes. These taxes could be around 50% or more. This would mean the estate taxes on the land could be around $250,000. They do not like this option, so they continue to look for other alternatives to achieve their goals.

Jack was a successful football star in his earlier days, which now puts him and his wife in the highest tax bracket (39.6%).

Jack and Diane decide to set up a charitable remainder trust (CRT) with the real estate. The wish to receive fixed annual payments, rather than variable payments from year to year. Thus, they have decided to set up a charitable remainder annuity trust (CRAT). With the minimum income distribution being 5% of trust principal, Jack and Diane will receive a $25,000 annual distribution from the CRAT. This is more than enough for life to go on.

Jack and Diane decide to name the local university as the charity to use to set up the CRT. After all, this is where Jack became a football star. Jack and his CPA have determined that the amount of charitable contribution deduction that they will get to claim on their tax return is $350,000. This will give them a tax savings of around $135,000.

In order to assure themselves that their son will be adequately provided for, Jack and Diane gift their son $20,000 ($10,000 each) each year. John then takes this money and purchases a life insurance policy for $500,000 on his dad with himself as a beneficiary. John now stands to inherit the same amount

that he would have received if he were to just have inherited the land. What's more is this $500,000 does not have to go through estate taxes because John owns the policy, not Jack. This saves John around $250,000 in estate taxes. This type of planning has essentially doubled John's inheritance, while giving Jack and Diane a current year tax benefit of $135,000.

Irrevocable Life Insurance Trust

What a lot of people do not realize is that life insurance proceeds become part of a deceased taxpayer's estate. Often times, taxpayers think their estate is too small to worry about estate taxes. Once insurance proceeds are thrown on top of other assets, it is very easy for an estate to be subject to estate taxes. It is not uncommon at all to see people with large life insurance policies, up to $1 million or more. Young people in the early stages of their wealth accumulation often fall into this category. Life insurance is very cheap for them, so they can afford a large policy. Also, more money would be needed for a spouse a child to survive during their lifetime, if a person should die at an early age. With estate possibly looming in the 50% to 60% range, your million dollar life insurance policy could cost you around $500,000 in estate taxes. Sure, you're still better off than with no insurance at all, but what if there was a way to make sure that the entire amount of insurance proceeds passed to your heirs?

An irrevocable life insurance trust (ILIT) is created to hold and own life insurance policies which enables the trust to keep the insurance proceeds out of the estate of the insured and his or her spouse. Once again, this is an irrevocable trust. That means that once it is set up, it can not be terminated. The

overwhelming benefit of an ILIT is that the insurance proceeds of the estate ultimately pass to the heirs tax free.

Let's say you have a taxable estate worth $1,000,000 after all exclusions. Your estate taxes are estimated to be around $350,000. You decide you want to purchase a $500,000 life insurance policy to help pay the taxes. You have two methods in which to purchase the policy.

Situation #1:
You purchase the life insurance policy and own it yourself. This adds another $500,000 to your taxable estate, or additional estate taxes of about $210,000. Thus, almost half of the insurance money winds up in the government's hands instead of your heirs.

Situation #2:
You can establish an irrevocable life insurance trust to hold and own the insurance policy. The proceeds from the policy ($500,000) will not be included in your estate. The trustee could take the insurance proceeds and purchase the assets from your taxable estate. Your heirs would then have enough liquid cash to pay the $350,000 in estate taxes without having to sell non-liquid assets. The trust now holds the assets that made up your estate. These assets can now be used to provide for the needs of your heirs.

One of the inherit disadvantages with any type of irrevocable trust is that it cannot be undone. We can, in some ways, get around this in regards to an irrevocable life insurance trust. Let's test our knowledge of the insurance industry. Term life insurance lasts for a specified term with an option to be renewed. If an ILIT was funded with a term policy rather that a whole life

policy, the policy payments can be stopped and the insurance will terminate. If the life insurance policy is terminated, the trust has essentially been terminated.

Asset Protection Trusts

As we have discussed many times, asset protection is one of the main components of the Secret Millionaire strategy. The main tools that are used to protect assets are corporations, limited partnerships, and limited liability companies. Each of these entities help shield personal assets from business creditors. They do not, however, protect an individual from personal claims, such as personal creditor claims and personal tort liability.

Offshore Asset Protection Trusts

When we talk about asset protection trusts, we are talking about protecting personal assets from personal liabilities. One of the most popular forms of this type of asset protection is the offshore asset protection trust (OAPT). An OAPT is basically a trust created under the laws of foreign jurisdictions that protect the assets in the trusts from future creditors. There are numerous foreign jurisdictions that have enacted favorable trust laws with the intent of attracting money in to its economy.

The OAPT has far more advantages when it comes to asset protection than domestic trust options. Domestic trusts do not allow grantor to set up trusts for the benefit of themselves, such as to insulate the grantor from creditors. In domestic asset protection trusts, which we will discuss shortly, laws are set up for the protection and benefit of the beneficiary. Offshore, laws are more

favorable to the grantor.

To be quite honest, you put a net of foreign laws between yourself and those who would like to have your hard-earned wealth without having to earn it. Now, I must emphasize that I am not an advocate from people being able to avoid their rightful responsibilities. What we are talking about here are frivolous claims, which we have discussed are out of control. I do not believe that an honest, hard-working individual must give up their life savings because they spill a cup of coffee on somebody.

Offshore asset protection trusts are very effective when it comes to protecting your hard-earned assets from these kinds of claims. Some of the benefits of OAPTs are:

- Minimal cooperation between foreign governments and U.S. courts
- Shorter statute of limitations in foreign jurisdictions which limit the time in which a frivolous lawsuit can actually be won.
- Foreign jurisdictions do not honor judgments levied in other jurisdictions. This means the creditor will have to bring a new lawsuit in the foreign country.
- Attempting to attach or levy assets contained in foreign OAPTs can be very time consuming and expensive.

The biggest hurdle to overcome in dealing OAPTs would be learning the laws of the country in which you are investing. Remember, their laws, just like ours, are always changing. Your trust is subject to the laws of the foreign jurisdiction, not the laws of the U.S. You must do your homework before investing.

Ask questions. Read about the experiences of others in the countries that you are considering. Obviously, this is a very specialized area of planning, so make sure you are getting experienced, competent advice.

Spendthrift Trusts

A spendthrift trust is one of the more popular domestic trusts used for asset protection. As mentioned earlier, domestic trusts cannot be set up for the self-serving benefit of the grantor. This basically means you cannot put your assets into a trust in the U.S. for the purpose of shielding those assets from your creditors. Spendthrift trusts are used to protect the interests of the trust beneficiaries. A spendthrift trust is called that because it contains a spendthrift provision in the trust document. A spendthrift provision states that the trust is intended to provide for the health, education and support of the trust beneficiaries. A typical spendthrift provision would read as follows:

No interest of any beneficiary in the income or principal of this trust shall be assigned, transferred, or otherwise encumbered in anticipation of future payment or be liable in any way for the beneficiaries' debts, liabilities, or obligations and shall not be subject to attachment.

Thus, a creditor of the beneficiary cannot attach his or her interest in a spendthrift trust. In other words, a creditor cannot get these assets. Once income is paid to the beneficiary, this now becomes a personal asset of the beneficiary and can be had by creditors.

Discretionary Trusts

Another common type of a domestic asset protection trust is a discretionary trust. In a discretionary trust the trustee has total discretion on distributions from the trust. Therefore, a creditor who has a judgment against a beneficiary cannot compel the trustee to make a distribution to the beneficiary. If the beneficiary doesn't get it, neither does the creditor.

It is important to note that spendthrift and discretionary trust, as well as other types of asset protection trusts, can be used in the same trust. Remember, these trusts will not guarantee that a creditor will not attempt to get these assets. However, you have now created another entity, or shield, in which the creditor will have to penetrate to get your assets. The time and expense of such a task will be an enormous obstacle that your creditors will have to overcome.

What are the advantages of trusts?

Hopefully, our discussion of the different types of trust has helped you to begin to answer this question already. Trusts can basically be set up to do anything you wish to do. Basically, trusts help solve your problems. Properly structured, trusts can help you do the following:

- Avoid probate
- Avoid publicity associated with probate
- Manage assets for your family in the event of your death
- Manage assets for your family if you were to become disabled

- Lower estate taxes
- Avoid creditors
- Provide for spouse
- Provide for children
- Provide for dependent parents
- Provide for charities
- Provide for non-family members
- Give you tremendous peace of mind

What price can you put on the advantages mentioned above? I sincerely doubt that anyone reading this book will answer no to any one of these benefits. Trusts provide for you and your loved ones future. Certain trusts give you the ability to "change your mind" if situations change later in life. Trusts give you the ability to decide how **you** want your assets to be managed and distributed.

What are the disadvantages of trusts?

Someone once said that for every action (advantage) there is an equal and opposite reaction (disadvantage). I have now proven that this is not necessarily true. While trust advantages are numerous, there are very few disadvantages.

Initially, trusts may be expensive. You must weigh the long-term costs of establishing a trust with the intended outcome you wish to achieve. Trusts may also have annual costs associated with maintaining and managing them. You may be faced with large amounts of paperwork or upkeep. You basically have to decide if managing your assets by your rules is worth the cost.

Ironically, trusts involve a certain degree of trust. You will need to choose a trustee who will follow your wishes and carry out your instructions the way you intended. In certain trusts, the trustee has a large degree of responsibility and discretion.

Always remember, irrevocable trusts are just that. There is no going back. Be sure you are certain about your goals and objectives.

In addition to these minor disadvantages, trusts may be subject to complex tax rules. Make certain that your financial professional or accountant will provide tax consulting service for the trust.

How do trusts compare with other legal entities?

A trust, like a corporation, limited partnership, and limited liability company, is a creature of law. Certain trusts file their own income tax returns and pay their own taxes. Most legal entities have their own business purpose such as renting property or retail sales. Added benefits to these business structures are asset protection, estate planning, and tax reduction. Trusts are set up for the purpose of asset protection, estate planning, and tax reduction.

Trusts offer the flexibility of tailoring them to meet your specific needs. As mentioned earlier, trusts have many different forms. There are insurance trusts, asset protection trusts, charitable trusts, and many more. Corporations, limited partnerships, and limited liability companies are not flexible at all. You have to conform your approach to the advantages of each different entity. Trusts can be created to accomplish any goal you have in mind. As such, they become an essential part of your overall Asset Security System. If you are

interested in setting up or learning more about any of the various types of trusts, call Profit Publishing Group, Inc. toll-free at 877.868.9742. As the late, great Supreme Court Justice Oliver Wendell Holmes stated, "Put not your trust in money, put your money in trust."

"Let him that would move the world, first move himself."
Socrates

CHAPTER IX
SECRET MILLIONAIRE TOOL #5:
RETIREMENT PLANS

The first step in becoming wealthy is making the decision to become wealthy. This may sound strange to many of you reading this because you may be thinking to yourself, "Of course I want to be wealthy, who doesn't?" To be quite honest, most people do not truly want to be wealthy. If they did, they would do the things that make people wealthy. Let me say right now, however, that I am not being callous when I say this. I'm simply being truthful.

Far too often, people will talk about things that they truly want to accomplish yet they are simply not willing to put forth what it is that is necessary to accomplish their objectives. For instance, I have heard people make the comment, "I would give anything to be able to shoot a golf score of 72." Without realizing it, they are lying to themselves. When they say that they are willing to do anything, they need to ask themselves whether they are willing to make golf a big enough priority in their life to spend the time, effort, energy, and of course, money, in order to become that good of a golfer. If they are not willing to do it, they need to admit this to themselves and concentrate on what it is that they really want to do.

My intention here is not to get up on a soapbox and preach to you about the problems of why people do not obtain what it is they set out to do, my intention is to make a point. Part of becoming wealthy is to make certain sacrifices. One of those sacrifices is to put off short-term pleasures in order to build up long-term wealth. Rarely is this seen more than in the area of retirement planning. In order to fully understand this complex area, it is crucial that you gain an understanding of the components. We'll start with the basics.

What is a retirement plan?

Perhaps in no other area of financial planning is the potential for accumulation of wealth greater than in retirement plans. Let me ask you, how many of you reading this book right now are currently participating in your employer's 401K plan? I usually get a very favorable response from this question at our seminars. Retirement plans, such as a 401K, are now almost as common a part of an employer's benefit package as health insurance. Why do you think the stock market has taken off over the last few years? More and more people now have the opportunity to invest than ever before. Kids right out of school have the ability to put back $100 per month or more for retirement. Now let me ask you, why do you participate in your company's 401K plan? Why do you have part of your hard-earned paycheck set aside? The answers to this question may vary, but most tend to fall around these main categories:

- Immediate tax savings
- Deferred tax growth
- Employer matching contributions
- Peace of mind with regard to building for your financial future

While there are certainly other benefits which we will get into in more detail later in this chapter, the above-mentioned characteristics of retirement plans provide the backbone for one of the most powerful wealth building tools available today.

To better illustrate this point, let's go through an example of exactly how a retirement plan can benefit its participants. Let's assume Bill incorporated his computer company. After weighing his investment options, he decides to set up a retirement plan through his corporation. Bill is the sole shareholder of the corporation and is its only employee. Macro-tech, Inc. is in the 34% corporate income tax bracket. Bill, himself, is in the 39.6% bracket.

Bill and his accountant determine he can put back $10,000 this year in his retirement plan. The corporation also can match $5,000 of this contribution.

How has this action given Bill the advantages mentioned above? Let's take a look.

Immediate Tax Savings #1: Macro-tech, Inc. gets to deduct the $15,000 from its taxable income in the current year. That will save the corporation $5,100.

Immediate Tax Savings #2: Bill, as an employee, does not report the $15,000 as taxable income in the current year, even though this retirement account is now in Bill's name. If the income had been paid to Bill personally to invest, he would have paid taxes of $5,940, leaving him only $9,060 to invest.

Deferred Tax Savings #1: When Bill pulls this money out at retirement, he will pay taxes in the year it comes out at the tax rate in place at that time. If Bill retires in a 28% tax bracket, he will pay taxes of $4200 when he pulls it out, as opposed to $5940 if the income were taxes currently.

Deferred Tax Savings #2: The income generated by the retirement plan will not be taxed until Bill pulls it out for retirement. If the $15,000 were to earn 10%, that would be $594 of taxes Bill could defer currently. If Bill happens to retire in a lower tax bracket, he has saved money once again. The very minimum benefit is a long-term interest free loan from the IRS.

How does it sound like Bill is doing so far? Notwithstanding the multitude of ancillary benefits that Bill has obtained by establishing his retirement plan, let's focus on the tax savings. This setup is what I refer to as a tax savings double play. Two benefits at once. A current year tax deduction coupled with deferred tax income sounds too good to be true. However, this tremendous opportunity is real and is currently being used by millions of America's most successful individuals. Now is the time for you to join them.

What are the different types of retirement plans?

As we begin our journey into learning about retirement plans, we must first identify the different types of plans. The first thing to understand is that we have *individual* and *business* plans. We'll begin by taking a look at individual plans.

Individual Retirement Accounts

A retirement plan in its most basic form is called an individual retirement account, or IRA. Traditionally, an IRA has been the most frequently used tool for retirement planning. An IRA is a personal savings plan that allows a taxpayer to accumulate money tax deferred until retirement. A taxpayer and his spouse can put up to $2,000 each into an IRA each year, assuming they meet the qualifications. Contributions to an IRA may or may not be deductible depending on specific circumstances. For our purposes here, we will assume that an IRA contribution does qualify as a deductible expense. Let's see how this works.

Fred and his wife, Wilma, are in their late thirties. Fred has worked at a rock quarry for the last ten years. Wilma has stayed home to take care of their little girl. Fred's company does not offer a retirement package to employees. Acting on some good advice, Fred establishes an IRA for both himself and Wilma and contributes $2,000 each for the current year. Fred and Wilma are in the 28% tax bracket. The $4,000 of deductible IRA contributions saved them $1,120 on their current year tax bill. Fred's IRA does well the following year and earns 20%. This income will not be taxed until Fred pulls it out at retirement. The bottom line here is that Fred has not only saved some tax dollars but he has put aside money to plan for a great retirement.

Roth IRA

The above is an example of retirement plans in their simplest form. As you can see, even at this stage they can be beneficial. At this point, I must bring up a new phenomenon called a Roth IRA. A Roth IRA is still limited to an annual contribution of $2,000. However, this contribution is not tax deductible. In our example above, Fred and Wilma would have saved nothing on their current year tax bill. That may sound bad, but there's good news. The income generated by the IRA is not taxed currently *or* when it is pulled out at retirement. That's right, the entire amount grows tax free, as opposed to tax deferred. This is a new concept and it is absolutely taking the country by storm. It is certainly something you need to take a look at and strongly consider becoming involved in.

Both the traditional IRA and the Roth IRA are individual plans. They are created by individuals like you and me. Businesses, however, have a few more options on creating retirement plans. These plans provide the opportunity to put back substantial amounts of money and receive a current year tax deduction through your business.

Retirement Plans for Businesses

I mentioned earlier that the two basic types of plans are individual and business. We've taken a brief look at individual plans, now let's take a look at retirement plans for businesses. The two basic types of retirement plans for businesses are qualified plans and non-qualified plans. At first, this may sound strange; qualified vs. non-qualified. Essentially, the distinction between the two is quite simple. Qualified plans are those plans which must comply with the special requirements of Section 401 of the Internal Revenue Code and are governed by the Employee's Retirement Income Security Act, known as "ERISA". Non-qualified plans are those that are not required to comply with the requirements of Section 401 and are not governed by ERISA. The real distinction is that qualified plans are what are known as "tax-advantaged", whereas non-qualified plans are not "tax-advantaged." It's that simple.

While this may sound like it's getting a little complex, it's really not that complicated. When terms like "ERISA" are thrown around however, people tend to wonder how everything works. To clear this up a little bit, let's take a look at what ERISA is all about.

What is ERISA?

The Employee's Retirement Income Security Act (ERISA) is a complex set of federal laws governing tax-advantaged retirement plans for employees of businesses. ERISA has been around since 1974 and has been revised by Congress numerous times. The ERISA laws are enforced by the Department of Labor and the IRS. Whenever you see the term "qualified plan," it means that it is an employee benefit plan governed by these ERISA rules.

One important function of the ERISA rules is to prohibit retirement plans from discriminating among employees. This means that plans can't favor business owners and officers of a business over other employees in granting tax-advantaged benefits. These prohibitions often make ERISA plans too expensive for typical small businesses. A common dilemma is often that a business can't afford to cover all of its employees in its plans, but wants the benefits for the owners. So now we need to determine how to deal with this dilemma.

While there are restrictions, the law grants some flexibility to owners. A company can place specific vesting requirements so that employees can be kept out of that company's retirement plan until they have stuck around long enough to be valuable to the business. This is a common practice among many smaller businesses with retirement plans.

The question we need to answer now is, which type of plan is best for you and your business? To answer that question, we need to know the alternatives.

What are the different types of qualified retirement plans?

There are several different types of retirement savings plans. Depending on the type of plan you choose, contributions can be made by the business, the employee or both. The tax advantages of having an ERISA governed or "qualified" plan are:

1) Contributions to an employee's retirement plan are usually tax-deductible expenses to the business, thus reducing its taxable income.
2) Contributions to a retirement plan are made with before-tax dollars rather than after-tax dollars. This reduces taxable income.

Money in retirement plans earns income without being taxed as long as it remains in the plan. Withdrawals from a plan can begin as early as age 55, but can be delayed until up until you reach age 70 1/2. These withdrawals are taxed at the participant's then current tax bracket, which is likely to be lower than when he or she was working.

It is important to understand that participants in retirement plans do not have to stay with the company until retirement age to get their benefits. Whether they leave voluntarily or not, they have a "vested" right to whatever they contributed to the plan through the date they leave. They might not be entitled to money contributed by their employer, however, unless they have worked a minimum number of years, often around four or five. And of course, they will have to reach retirement age before the right to collect the benefits kicks in.

Qualified Retirement Plans

Because qualified retirement plans comply with section 401 of the Internal Revenue Code, they have tax advantages that non-qualified retirement plans do not. The main advantages are:

- Employer contributions are tax deductible to the company.
- Employer contributions are tax deferred to the employee.
- Earnings in the plan are tax deferred.

As stated previously, qualified retirement plans must comply with the Internal Revenue Code. Some of the characteristics that a plan must contain in order to comply with the Code are as follows:

- The plan cannot discriminate between employees.
- Contributions to the plan can be made by both the employer and the employee.
- The plan must be for the exclusive benefit of the employees.
- The plan must contain minimum vesting standards.
- The plan must be permanent.

There are two main types of qualified retirement plans. They are a defined benefit plan and a defined contribution plan. The differences in these two plans are really quite simple to understand.

Defined Contribution Plan: Defines the amount that is contributed to the plan each year for each participant's individual account. For instance, a defined contribution plan may promise to contribute $2000 per year or 10% of someone's salary to each individual's specific account. The amount to be paid at retirement varies according to the performance of the plan.

Defined Benefit Plan: Pays a specific benefit at a certain age. For instance, a defined benefit plan may promise participants a lifetime payment of $1000 per month upon reaching age 65. The employer must take the steps necessary to ensure that the plan will be adequately funded to provide the defined benefit at the time it becomes payable.

Each of these plans have their own special benefits. Let's take a closer look at each.

Defined Contribution Plans

The defined-contribution plan is the most popular type of corporate retirement plan, because it is usually funded by the employee rather than the business. Here, part of an employee's pay is deducted and put into an investment account.

In most defined contribution plans, the employer decides the contribution percentage for everyone. The corporation contributes a lump sum to the plan, which allocates to each employee's account based on his or her compensation. Plan contributions can be allocated disproportionately to slightly favor owners over employees.

As with most retirement plans, the account balance in a defined contribution plan upon retirement will depend on how much has been contributed and how well the fund's investments have performed. No fixed lump sum or monthly payments are promised to a plan participant, as is the case with a defined benefit plan.

Defined contribution plans are the most commonly used plans. Some examples of defined contribution plans include:

- Money Purchase Plans
- Profit Sharing Plans
- Thrift Plans
- 401(K)
- Target Benefit Plans
- Employee stock ownership plan (ESOP)

The size of a participant's account balance in a defined contribution plan de-

pends on the amount of contributions both the employee and the employer and on the plan's investment performance. The benefits of this plan are not guaranteed. Poor investment performance will yield smaller retirement benefits.

The current maximum amount that can be contributed to a defined contribution plan is $30,000. Remember, this contribution is deductible by the employer and tax deferred to the employee.

Defined Benefit Plan

The traditional corporate retirement plan is called a defined-benefit plan. This type of plan promises a specific monthly benefit for the life of the participant upon retirement. With a defined benefit plan, each participant knows how much he or she will get every month. In general, the longer an employee is with the company, the larger the monthly benefit.

Deciding on what type of plan is best for you and your business is a very important matter. I highly recommend speaking with a pension specialist if you are contemplating establishing a corporate retirement plan.

Defined benefit plans do not have specific individual account balances in the names of the plan participants. Remember, the amount of benefits to be paid is fixed. Formulas based on actuarial assumptions that include things such as mortality rates are used to determine how the plan invests in order to meet its defined obligation. There are no limits on the amounts of employer contributions that can be made to a defined benefit plan. The amount of contribution can be whatever is required to achieve the defined benefit. This allows for a much larger potential contribution than the $30,000 limit of defined contribution plans.

Defined benefit plans are advantageous to small employers who are extremely profitable and whose employees are older (45-55). Employees who are older have a much shorter time to save for retirement. If they

were limited to the prescribed contribution amounts that a defined contribution plan allows for, they may not have enough time to build up that retirement nest egg they desire. A defined benefit plan places no limits on how large a contribution can be made in a single year. The amount of contribution is whatever is needed to achieve the desired retirement benefit.

The major downfall of defined benefit plans is the costs associated with them. Because they a based on complex actuarial computations, defined benefit plans are more expensive to implement than defined contribution plans.

How do I withdraw money out of my retirement plan?

One question I seem to always be asked is how someone can pull money out of their retirement plan. Too many times, people are looking for me to be able to teach them some miraculous way to take money out of their plan and never pay taxes. Unfortunately, that's not going to happen.

Money taken out of any retirement plan becomes taxable income. There are a few exceptions to this such as loans, which are possible only from certain types of plans. Withdrawals are taxed at your personal income tax bracket in the year you take out the money. Hopefully, when you retire, your income tax bracket will be lower than when you were working, which could mean a drop from as much as 39.6% to as low as 15%. This will really depend on your overall financial situation at the time. If you don't meet all of the rules at the time you pull money out of your retirement account, you will be subject not only to income tax on the withdrawals but to a special penalty tax as well.

Be careful not to get the idea that the withdrawal rules are any easier than the rest of the overly complicated tax law on retirement plans. That is certainly not the case. There are different rules for just about every type of plan when it comes to the issue of withdrawals. If you are currently participating in a retirement plan, it will certainly pay to check with a tax or pension specialist before taking any money out of a retirement

plan. For information on innovative and aggressive retirement plan strategies, call Profit Publishing Group, Inc. toll-free at 877.868.9742 to schedule an appointment with a specialist in the field of pension and retirement planning.

Corporate Plan Withdrawals

Distribution rules for corporate plans are more liberal than with other plans. For example, in a corporate plan you can start taking out money without penalty as early as age 55. Before that age, the 10% premature penalty tax kicks in. Like all other retirement savings plans, you must start withdrawing funds by age 70 1/2. There is an exception to this rule for those who continue to work past age 70 1/2. In this instance, you can put off withdrawals as long as you don't own more than 5% of the stock of the corporation. A minimum amount must be withdrawn each year after attaining 70 1/2, based on your life expectancy under IRS tables. For futher assistance, speak with a qualified pension specialist.

Non-qualified Retirement Plans

As stated previously, non-qualified retirement plans do not comply with section 401 of the Internal Revenue Code. Therefore, they are subject to less regulation than qualified retirement plans. Employers can discrimi-nate in favor of key employees. This is the main reason non-qualified plans are put in place. They are often used to retain key employees in positions of power and influence.

The downside of non-qualified retirement plans is that contributions to the plan are not deductible by the employer until included in the employee's taxable income.

What are the advantages of retirement plans?

This is an area I feel needs repeating. Perhaps is no other area of finan-

cial planning is the potential accumulation of wealth greater than in retirement plans. Retirement plans offer the employer a current tax deduction. Retirement plans offer the employee deferred tax income along with deferred tax growth. The Secret Millionaire Mindset says why not take advantage of both benefits at the same time.

Let's re-emphasize the advantages of retirement plans.

- Employer contributions are deductible by the employer.
- Employee contributions are tax deferred.
- Investment earnings of the plan are tax deferred.
- Employers can make matching contributions to the employee.
- Peace of mind for your retirement years.

Take a look at the facts. Most American's wealth and net worth is achieved through the use of retirement plans. Congress knows this. There is no guarantee that the rules in place today for retirement plans will be the same rules we are playing by twenty, ten, or even five years from now. If you are 40 years old, the IRS is basically giving you an interest free loan for 25 years. Think of the power of these three concepts:

- Current tax deductions
- Deferred taxes on contributions
- Interest free growth

Those words are music to the Secret Millioniare's Ears.

What are the disadvantages of retirement plans?

Someone in some other line of work once said, "For every action there is an equal and opposite reaction." I don't believe that is the case for retirement plans. Anytime I talk on a given subject I like to use "advantages

and disadvantages" comparisons. It makes perfect sense. If anything or idea was so good, why doesn't everybody do it. I try to give both sides of the story.

Retirement plans really only have one side, and that side is good. After many hours of thinking, I have come up with only two disadvantages to retirement plans.

- It actually takes current money to set them up.
- The funds in retirement plans are generally not accessible, without penalty, until retirement.

I know the idea of taking your money and putting it in another savings account that you own just to avoid paying the IRS several thousand dollars this year is not that appealing to some people. In my opinion, if you have the money, there is no better place to watch that money grow that in a retirement plan.

How do retirement plans provide asset protection?

We always come back to our three fundamental objectives of the Secret Millionaire.

1. Asset Protection
2. Estate Planning
3. Tax Reduction

What about retirement plans? Do they accomplish all three goals, or just one? The assets in tax-qualified retirement plans are generally protected from creditors. When we mention tax-qualified we are talking about ERISA. The Employee Retirement Income Security Act of 1974, or ERISA, is a federal law specifically aimed at providing protection to participants in employee benefit plans. The Supreme Court has stated that creditors cannot reach ERISA qualified pension plans.

It is important to note that just because there are precedents that protect retirement plans, that will not automatically stop an attorney from attempting to go after those assets. The key here is that your plan must be set up properly. The law is open. If the pension plan does not follow the strict guidelines of ERISA and possibly section 401 of the Internal Revenue Code then creditors may potentially be able to get into retirement and pension plans. Make sure your retirement plan is set up properly.

How can retirement plans provide estate planning?

In simple terms, retirement plans provide estate planning by growing the size of your estate tremendously. Have you ever looked at compounding interest tables? Do you realize how powerful compounding interest can be?

Money doubles every 7.2 years assuming a 10% rate of return. As we all know a 10% rate of return is not a guarantee, but it is well below what we have been averaging for the past few years. Let's look at an example of this.

Assume Harry is 50 years old. Harry has recently started his own business and is interested in starting a retirement plan. Harry believes he has the resources to contribute $5000 to his retirement plan every year. Remember, money doubles every 7.2 years assuming a 10% rate of return. How many seven year periods does Harry have between age 50 and 65. It looks as if the answer is two, but there are actually 9 full seven year periods and 6 partial periods between ages 50 and 65.

Age 50-56	1 period
Age 51-57	2 periods
Age 52-58	3 periods
Age 53-59	4 periods
Age 54-60	5 periods
Age 55-61	6 periods

Age 56-62	7 periods
Age 57-63	8 periods
Age 58-64	9 periods

The remaining funding years (ages 59 through 64) would be partial years in relation to the doubling feature. Let's assume Harry put in $5000 at age 50. If he did not contribute again, the retirement plan would have around $23,000 in it by age 65 (assuming a 10% rate of return.) Now, if Harry contributes $5000 every year between the ages of 50 and 65, his investment of $80,000 would be worth almost $200,000.

This example assumes three important factors that can all be improved upon:

1. Investment starts at age 50.
2. Contributions of only $5000 per year are made.
3. The retirement plan earns only 10% per year.

What would happen if Harry were only 30 years old and decided to put back $5000 per year until age 65. His $180,000 investment over 36 years would be worth about $1,650,000. What if Harry put in more?

Clearly, any estate plan has the goal of providing the largest estate possible for your heirs. Retirement plans are a very efficient way of achieving this goal.

How can retirement plans help me reduce my tax bill?

If you have learned anything in this chapter it is that retirement plans reduce current taxes. This occurs in three ways.

1. Employee contributions are tax deferred.
2. Employer contributions are deductible.
3. Investment in the plan grows tax deferred.

In our example above, Harry put back $5000 per year in a retirement plan. If Harry is in the 28% tax bracket, he saved $1400 on income taxes each year he contributed. Remember, this does not include state income tax savings. Also remember that many of you reading this book will be in a much higher tax bracket. If Harry's company also made a matching contribution of $5000 per year, that $5000 is deducted by Harry's company, once again, saving him money. What's more, this matching contribution is not subject to income taxes in the current year to Harry. That's right. That income to Harry is tax deferred. The growth of the plan is also tax deferred.

Remember our talk of different types of income back in the tax planning section of this book? Well, we have just converted earned income (the worst kind) to tax deferred income (one of the best kinds). We have definitely begun to defend ourselves against the IRS.

How can I learn more about and establish a retirement plan?

Pension and retirement plans can be great tools in preparing for your retirement. Not only can the contributions be tax-deductible, but the dollars inside the plan enjoy tax-deferred income growth. Through the miracle of compounding, you could find yourself with several million dollars in a relatively short time. Another great thing about pensions is their protection from both lawsuits and bankruptcy. A pension plan can be an integral part of your overall plan. As always, if you plan on implementing this plan, seek assistance. It will save you far more than it ever costs. The best way to do that is to call Profit Publishing Group, Inc. toll-free at 877.868.9742 and ask to be scheduled to speak with a pension and retirement planning specialist. It will put you well on your way to becoming a Secret Millionaire.

"Keep company with those who make you better."
English Proverb

CHAPTER X
THE SECRET MILLIONAIRE'S
SECRET WEAPON

A key principle which must be followed in order to achieve phenomenal success in any endeavor is to surround yourself with those who make you better. This is essential to your overall success. Throughout this book, I have made reference over and over again to the importance of consulting with a group of qualified tax accountants, attorneys, and/or other professionals. This is perhaps the best advice I could possibly give you. Will this cost you some money? Absolutely. More importantly however, it will not cost you anywhere near as much money as it would, had you not sought this advice.

Much of the work involved in setting up and administering your asset security system is relatively straightforward and routine. Any knowledgeable and motivated person can effectively accomplish much of this himself or herself. But one thing that you must realize is that you *will* need assistance from others from time to time. Some of the decisions you must make will involve complex areas of law and/or taxation and are best directed to qualified professionals. Other decisions will require an integration of business, legal, and financial savvy and are best left to the assistance of a smart small business attorney. The bottom line is to seek out the assistance of those who are experienced in these areas. This chapter is designed to help you in your search.

What is a "Master Mind" Team?

As a "secret millionaire", one of the most important steps you could possibly take to preserve the wealth you have accumulated is to build your "Master Mind" team. This will consist of those professionals who will give you the much needed assistance in areas which require more specialized knowledge.

> *Just as you would not keep just one tool in your toolbox, you cannot keep just one member on your "mastermind" team.*

This will include a vast array of different professionals, basically specialized tools for your toolbox. You will need several members for your team because you never know which one will be the best for any given situation. Just as you would not keep just one tool in your toolbox, you cannot keep just one member on your "master mind" team.

In building your team, here are a few suggestions on who you will need:

1)   Attorney;
2)   Accountant;
3)   Financial Professional;
4)   Insurance Agent;
5)   Real Estate Agent;
6)   Stockbroker;
7)   Spouse;
8)   Pension Specialist;
9)   Others.

While all of the above team members are important to your overall success, I

want to pay particular attention to the two which will be most beneficial to you in establishing and administering your plan. These are your attorney and your tax advisor. Before we talk about these important team members, you need to understand about an important pitfall that many people are exposed to. By understanding this, you will be less likely to fall into this trap.

Do not fall into the trap of thinking that you can just save the money and do it all yourself. Too many times people end up doing as one financial strategist refers to in his books as *"tripping over pennies on their way to dollars."* If you want to save the big money over the long haul, a "master mind" team can be the quintessential ingredient to your overall success. But the key is in setting up your team. I have included here a section on forming that team so that you can be further along on your mission to become a "secret millionaire" and so that you will be that much closer to having the things which you most want to have.

How do you find a good attorney?

One of the most important members of your team will be your attorney. No one member plays as large a role in the overall success of your operations as does the attorney when it comes to pure business and legal decisions. For this reason, it is imperative that you find an attorney who will be an asset to your organization and not a hindrance. Of course, I suggest that you make the decision to utilize the services of my company, Profit Publishing Group, Inc. to help you implement your plan. You can contact a representative to assist you by calling toll-free at 877.868.9742.

While the information and services provided by Profit Publishing Group, Inc.

are indeed beneficial, it is also advisable to seek local professional assistance with your situation. This is not in lieu of the professionals at Profit Publishing Group, Inc., rather, it is in conjunction with that portion of your team.

This section is designed to help you figure out the best way to find a good attorney-member of your team. The cost of placing a lawyer on retainer is cost-prohibitive for most people. Even when dealing with an attorney on an issue-by-issue basis, fees can add up swiftly, sometimes too swiftly for legal advice to be affordable except for the most important and most pressing issues. Just as with individuals, more and more individuals are trying to at least partially close this legal affordability gap by doing as much of their own work as possible. Oftentimes, doing this work yourself can save you some money. Other times, it makes sense to briefly consult with a lawyer at an interim stage, or have the paperwork reviewed upon completion. The key is being able to distinguish between what you should do yourself and what you should have someone help you with.

Depending on the size of your estate and the complexity of your legal needs, the next step you are likely to take is to find a competent and cooperative attorney who can assist you with your various legal concerns. Obviously, you are not searching for a lawyer who will take over *all* of your decision-making and running of your estate. That could cost an absolute fortune if you were paying this person on an hourly basis. Besides that, it would be unnecessary in all but the most complicated situations. What you really need is to find an attorney who can be a part of your overall team so that he or she can assist you with the more pressing concerns only.

It's important to understand when looking for a lawyer, that you do not need

a high-dollar, big-firm corporate lawyer for all of your legal issues. For many of the legal needs, a lawyer is a lawyer is a lawyer. That is not to minimize the value of a good lawyer, but their services should be retained for only the most specialized legal work. In today's legal market, there is an abundance of lawyers who are more than willing to work with you, many times even in unorthodox payment situations. Generally, you may not want a lawyer who works with high dollar estates. Two main reasons for this are that they will probably deal with issues that are much different from your particular estate planning concerns and they will most definitely charge you high dollar estate planning fees.

When searching for a good attorney, refrain from starting off your search with advertisements, legal directories, or the phone book. Unfortunately, lawyer referral services operated by state bar associations are every bit as unhelpful. These sources too many times merely supply the names of lawyers who have signed up for that particular service. One of the inherent problems with this is that these services simply rely on the attorney's word that they have the necessary qualifications.

The better approach is to speak with people in the community who you respect or who have the same or similar needs. Many times at our seminars, we ask people to stand up and introduce themselves to the people around them. Later, we will ask them to go out and meet someone else that they have not had the opportunity to meet. One of the main reasons that we do this is so that they can learn from others in their area about valuable resources. Ask these people about their lawyer(s) and how they feel about the quality of their work. If you speak with five to ten different people, it is highly likely that you will come away with some great information.

An additional source is to talk with other people such as bankers, accountants, insurance agents, real estate brokers, and others who may be able to provide the names of lawyers they feel comfortable and confident with in their own financial and estate planning concerns. One other source worth mentioning is to speak with friends, relatives, or even business associates within your own company who may also have names of possible attorneys to help you with your particular situation.

For most of your legal issues, you will not need to seek out an absolute specialist in their field. However, what if you do have a very technical legal question? Should you immediately seek out the services of a specialist? Generally, the answer to this is no. One good approach is to seek out a sort of assistant for identifying your issues. An example of this may be a lawyer who specializes in general practice who could at least identify your issue(s) and then determine whether or not you need a specialist.

When it comes to legal matters, there is no substitute for knowledge. There are some really good companies out there who hold seminars outlining various legal entities and assisting you with their implementation. Perhaps the best at doing this is Profit Publishing Group, Inc. which holds seminars on business and legal entities. They specialize in setting up legal entities and assisting with questions about the operation of these entities. If you are interested in their services, you can call the company toll-free at 877.868.9742 and ask to speak with an entity planning representative. One of the things that makes this company unique is that all plans are overseen by attorneys rather than trying to implement a one size fits all plan. The company specializes in taking complex legal and tax issues and making them understandable and easily implemented. This is a great way to deal with your legal concerns in a very cost-efficient

manner.

In the event that you decide to seek out a specialist for a more complicated legal matter, there are a few issues which you must pay particular attention to. After you have acquired the names of a few key prospects, don't wait around until a legal crisis occurs before establishing your initial contact with a lawyer. If you put the contact off until things are chaotic, you may not have sufficient time to find a lawyer who will work with you at an affordable price. In fact, it's extremely possible that you may end up settling for the first available person at a moment's notice. This almost always results in an unfavorable situation where you will pay too much for too little.

I learned this the hard way in a non-legal area when I was building my home. I contracted the project myself and was responsible for lining up all of the subcontractors. After being strung along by one of these subs, I was left in a position where I needed the work done ASAP. I called around and found the first available person to handle the job and was rather dissatisfied with the end result. I blame myself for this unfortunate situation because I let myself get into a situation where I had almost no choice but to take the first person available. In retrospect, it seems logical that I would not get the optimal results. If this person was available immediately, this should have told me something. They don't have any work. Why is that? Even if you are able to get a top-notch professional to do the job, if you wait until the last minute you will certainly pay for it.

When you do contact a lawyer, state your intentions in advance. Tell them that you are looking for someone who is willing to give you guidance, get you pointed in the right direction as needs arise, and to tackle those important legal

issues which you may find yourself faced with. In exchange for this, let the attorney know that you are more than willing to pay in a fair and prompt fashion. If they seem agreeable to this arrangement, ask to come to their office for a face-to-face meeting to get acquainted. Many lawyers will not charge you for this initial consultation. However, I have always found that it is a good idea to at least offer to pay them for their services. You want to establish from the get-go that while you only need them for specific issues, you are certainly not looking for a free ride. As an attorney myself, I can assure you that most attorneys don't mind talking to you briefly about inconsequential matters, but when it starts interfering with their making a living, it becomes a different matter.

Once you go in to meet with the lawyer, state your intentions again that you are looking for more of a legal advisor, a coach if you will, to assist you with legal concerns. Let me warn you right now that many lawyers will find this a bit unattractive, this whole idea of helping you in piecemeal fashion. If they seem especially uninterested, thank them for their time and move on. At this meeting, you will also want to discuss additional issues such as fees. It is sometimes an uncomfortable subject to bring up, but let me assure you that it is nowhere near as uncomfortable as bringing it up too far down the road.

Dealing with the issue of fees, it is always best to get a clear understanding of how fees will be imposed and calculated. An example of this might occur when your lawyer gives general legal advice from time to time or perhaps steers you in the right direction for a good legal source. The question now is: how will you be billed for this information? Some lawyers will bill a flat amount for a call or conference. Others will bill to the nearest time interval. Common time intervals are six, ten, or twenty minutes. When I was with a private firm, the standard practice was to bill in six-minute increments. The premise with this practice was that it takes at least six minutes to do anything once you document it in detail for billing purposes. The most important thing is to understand whatever billing system is in place.

The beginning of your relationship is the most critical time to develop the understanding of the billing process. To do this, ask the attorney specifically what it will cost for the job. If you feel that the amount is too much, don't hesitate to negotiate with the attorney. Ask for some alternative scenarios as well.

It is always a good idea to get all fee arrangements in writing. Any lawyer should understand this completely. The reason for this is that the written document will evidence a clear meeting of the minds on the issue. This becomes especially important when dealing with a larger job. The fact is, in many states the law requires that agreements between lawyers and clients be in writing if the fee is expected to be in excess of $1,000. I personally

> *...I would rather have it and not need it than need it and not have it.*

ally feel that it is advisable to get the agreement in writing even if the amount falls below this level. As I stated earlier in the book, there is a simple rule which I like to follow which is: ***I would rather have it and not need it than need it and not have it.***

There are a few standard methods which lawyers use to bill their clients. To better equip you in your dealings with attorneys, it is important for you to understand what these methods are. The primary methods are as follows:

1)   By the hour;

2)   Flat fee for a specific job;

3)   Contingent fee based upon settlement amounts or winnings;

4)   Retainer.

To give you a better understanding of these methods, let's take a look at them on an individual basis.

By the Hour: In most parts of the country, competent legal services are available for your business at a rate of $150-$250 per hour. Some of the newer attorneys who are still in the developmental stages of their practices may be available for paperwork review, legal research, and other types of legal work at lower rates. The only way to find out for sure is to ask.

Flat fee for a specific job: In this type of arrangement, you would pay the agreed-upon amount for a given project. The amount you pay will be regardless of how much or how little time is spent on the project by the lawyer. When you first begin working with a lawyer and are concerned about hourly costs soaring out of control, it is perhaps a good idea to negotiate a flat fee for a specific job. An example of this might be in a situation where a lawyer draws up a real estate purchase agreement for a set fee, or reviews and finalizes a buy-sell agreement for a flat fee, e.g. $500. This is a good arrangement.

Contingent fee based upon settlement amounts or winnings: This is the type of fee predominantly used in personal injury, products liability, and fraud and discrimination type cases, where a lawsuit is likely to be filed. In this instance, the lawyer would receive a percentage of the recovery in the event

that you win the case, but would receive nothing in the event that you lose. You may ask yourself why an attorney would take a case knowing full well that he may not get paid if you were to lose. You must understand however, that in the event that you do win the case, the lawyer will be paid handsomely. This pay will be in the neighborhood of 33-40% of the amount of the judgment. Since most business legal needs involve advice and assistance with drafting documentation, a contingency normally makes little sense. Notwithstanding this, if your business becomes involved in a personal injury claim or a lawsuit involving fraud, unfair competition, or an infringement of a patent or copyright, you may decide to explore the possibility of this type of fee arrangement.

Retainer: A select few individuals can afford to pay relatively modest amounts on a yearly basis to keep an estate planning or tax lawyer on retainer for ongoing phone or in-person consultations for routine matters during the year. This may run anywhere from $1,000 to $2,000. Of course, you must realize that your retainer won't cover a full-blown legal crisis. It may however, take care of any routine contract and other legal paperwork preparation and review throughout the year.

If you ever have any questions and/or concerns about an attorney's bill or the quality of his or her services, it is important that you voice those concerns. Acquiring legal assistance is just like purchasing any other consumer service. If you feel dissatisfied with any portion, you should seek a reduction in your bill or make it clear that the work needs to be redone to your satisfaction. Be reasonable about this. If you are in the wrong and feel that the attorney should have been able to get results for you that are simply unrealistic, deal with it. You should voice your concerns in the event that you feel that you were not

given adequate representation, not for failing to accomplish your desired results. If the attorney operates a well-run business, they should have no problem whatsoever dealing with your concerns in a positive and timely manner. If you are unable to get an acceptable response from that lawyer, find another one as soon as possible. If you do change attorneys, you are entitled to get your important documents back from the first lawyer.

In the event that you are to discharge your attorney, you may still feel that you have been unjustly wronged. If you are unable to come to an acceptable resolution to your problem, write to the client grievance office of the state bar association for the state in which the incident occurred. Another tip is to send a copy of the letter to the attorney. Oftentimes, a phone call to the attorney from this office tends to bring about the desired outcome.

There is one final thought I want to leave you with in regard to choosing a lawyer. It is crucial that you pay special attention to the rapport between you and your attorney. Keep in mind, you are looking for someone to guide and assist you in a manner that shows they are working *with* you. In many instances, it is best to trust your instincts and find a lawyer whose personality and business philosophies mesh with your own.

How do you find a good tax advisor?

Becoming proficient in the area of taxation is a huge task. To truly master all of the tax information applicable to you is almost impossible. Besides that, after you spend all your time trying to learn everything there is to know, you won't have time to be effective in your day to day activities. The good news is that you don't have to become an absolute expert in the field of taxation in

order to preserve your wealth for yourself and your family. Once you are equipped with a firm base level of knowledge, it is more advisable to find a good tax advisor. This person will become a key ingredient in your overall success and should become a part of your Master Mind team.

There are many different types of tax advisors out there to choose from. One problem however, is that the tax field is somewhat unregulated which suggests that you need to be careful. You need to find someone who really *is* an expert rather than someone who merely claims to be an expert.

What you are really looking for is someone who is experienced in helping people in your particular situation rather than someone who tends to offer a one size fits all plan. At the same time, there is seldom any need to seek the assistance of a CPA with one of the Big Six public accounting firms for your day to day issues.

Ideally, you need a professional who understands the type of situation in which you are involved. When it comes to matters of estate planning and the tax consequences related to structuring your estate, I recommend that you speak with a tax attorney. Typically, tax attorneys are the best bet on taking care of your specific needs when it comes to implementing the various estate planning and wealth preservation strategies.

While tax attorneys are the best when it comes to structuring your estate, when it comes to tax advisors, you will also need someone who can assist you in filing various tax returns. The following is a list of some of the tax professionals, including tax attorneys, who may be of assistance to you:

1) <u>A Tax Return Preparer</u>: Persons who refer to themselves as tax return preparers are not licensed through the IRS. The reason for this is that there is no requirement for such license. You can think what you want about the lack of formalized testing or licensing program. Some states impose their own requirements but most simply allow anyone to do it. This refers to both private individuals and also to the larger tax return preparation chains. These folks may be extremely knowledgeable about the subject of taxes or they may not be, you take your chances. As such, be careful.

2) <u>An Enrolled Agent</u>: An enrolled agent is a person who is licensed by the IRS as a tax preparer and advisor. In order to obtain this license, the person must pass a test administered by the IRS or by having at least five years of experience working for the IRS. In the United States, there are over 20,000 enrolled agents who provide not only tax assistance but sometimes even bookkeeping and accounting services as well. Of the tax pros available out there, enrolled agents are typically the least expensive.

3) <u>A Tax Attorney</u>: A tax attorney can oftentimes be the most expensive source of tax assistance but can also be the most valuable. A tax attorney is one who has chosen to specialize in the area of taxation as it relates to individuals and more specifically, to legal entities such as corporations, trusts, partnerships, LLCs, and retirement plans. Many times, tax attorneys will have attained an advanced law degree in the area of taxation or have received a tax-specific certification from a state bar association, though many states do not specifically grant this type of certification. These professionals should be retained in the event that you find yourself with a serious tax problem, require legal representation in court, or have a legal

problem with the IRS. They may also be of great assistance for complex tax and estate planning issues.

4) <u>A Certified Public Accountant (CPA)</u>: Finally, we have our friends the CPAs. CPAs are licensed and regulated by each state and are required to pass an extensive examination prior to obtaining their license. While this is similar to attorneys, I like to think that the bar exam is much more difficult than the CPA exam. This may have something to do with the fact that I passed the bar exam but never took the CPA exam. In any event, these are licensed professionals who perform sophisticated accounting and business tax work and tax preparation. They can be some of your greatest allies when it comes to business tax advice but are generally not as aggressive as tax attorneys when dealing with the IRS. It is my personal opinion that a CPA should be a part of your team as well as an attorney.

Tax professionals can be of tremendous assistance in many key areas. For this reason, it is important to choose a good member for your team. While there are several ways to choose a good tax professional, asking someone from the IRS for their suggestion is not your best resource. One of the best possible ways to find a good tax pro is to ask other people if they know someone. Obviously, there is more to it than simply asking someone else but this is a great place to start. If you can get the names of at least four or five to speak with, you can take it from there. The information you learned in choosing an attorney is applicable here as well. Make sure to find someone who you feel both comfortable and confident with.

In addition to asking others for referrals, look for advertisements. You should

take these advertisements with a grain of salt. As with all advertisements, those promoting the services of a tax advisor will paint a picture of a top notch professional whether that is the case or not. Another source will be the local bar associations and CPA societies. These names are usually given on a rotation basis from their list so you need to understand that this is not a recommendation or certification of competence. It is your responsibility to decide who you will use for your tax needs so make sure that you feel good about your decision.

Another item to be addressed is the fees associated with tax advice. Tax professionals aren't cheap, but neither is the lack of tax advice. It is important to realize that the fees involved in obtaining sound tax assistance as a part of your investment in your estate. A good tax professional can save you far more than they ever charge you. With that in mind, let's take a look at tax fees.

It is always a good idea to develop a clear understanding of how any fees will be imposed as soon as possible. Specifically, you need to know if fees will be charged on an hourly basis or whether services will be performed on a flat fee basis. The most common type of billing practice amongst professionals is to charge hourly. These fees can range anywhere from $25 to $250 per hour, depending on what type of tax professional you use (enrolled agents as the low, top CPAs and tax attorneys as the high).

You will remember that we said it is important to get things in writing when establishing your relationship with your attorney. This is also the case when dealing with your tax professional. You should ask for a written agreement *before* any work is done so that all parties know exactly where they stand.

This will become especially important should a dispute arise.

Remember also, that expenses are almost always negotiable. If you don't want to pay a large fee, voice your feelings. This is a problem that many people find themselves in. They don't want to pay so much but they never ask to pay less. Trust me, no one is going to reduce the bill for someone who seems happy paying the current fees. If you don't like the situation you're in, you have to do something about it.

SUMMARY

Building your Master Mind Team is one of the most critical ingredients to your overall success. When dealing with an issue of this importance, it is essential that you spend a little time making the decisions as to who will become a part of this team. Top legal, tax, and trust professionals are not cheap, but they can be worth their weight in gold when used properly. Above all, make sure that you find members for your team who you feel both comfortable and confident with. Always remember that the money you spend on top-level assistance is not an expense, it is an investment. For more information on how you can

> *Top legal, tax, and trust professionals are not cheap, but they can be worth their weight in gold when used properly.*

assemble a top-notch team of professionals, call the best in the business, Profit Publishing Group, Inc. toll-free at 877.868.9742. Call today!

"Conviction is worthless unless it is converted into conduct."
Thomas Carlyle

Chapter XI
The Secret Millionaire's Call to Action

When it comes to being a Secret Millionaire, this quote at the top of the page has always had special significance for me. Too often, I hear people talking about their ideals and convictions as if they would die for these. However, when it comes right down to it, they aren't really doing anything about it. It often turns out that these people who are espousing these principles are failing to abide by them themselves. If Thomas Carlyle had been a Secret Millionaire he may have made the quote read, "Secret Millionaire principles are worthless unless converted into action."

In many ways, I believe that this is the most important chapter in the book. Not because it contains the most crucial information on legal entities or the inner workings of your asset security system, but because it covers the most quintessential ingredient to your success. If you lack this portion, your success will be greatly limited. That essential element is *action.*

Understand, I am in no way minimizing the importance of learning about specific subjects. Gaining this knowledge is one of the most important undertakings a person could apply themselves to. My belief in this is evidenced by the fact that I have dedicated my life to the production of educational tools which enable people to gain this valuable knowledge. But I need to ask you a question. If you have all the information, yet fail to act upon it, how much good does it do you?

> *If you have all the information, yet fail to act upon it, how much good does it do you?*

Think about it. What does that tell you? Does that mean that there is no need for knowledge? Of course not! The thing you need to get a handle on is the way to balance these issues.

The best way to illustrate this point is to take a look at an example that I go through in my live seminars. During the seminar I will ask the students to raise their hands if they: 1) have children that they are putting through college right now; 2) have put their children through college in the past; or 3) put themselves through college. I have the students keep their hands up through the next question which is: how many of you deducted that expense? Invariably, nearly every hand in the room goes down.

The next question is one of the most telling. Why not? Why aren't you deducting these expenses? Understand that there are specific restrictions on whether or not these expenses are deductible. Too many times however, people fail to deduct things that they could have deducted.

When I ask people why they neglected to take the deduction, the answer is usually because they didn't know about it. They simply did not know that they could take this deduction. This is the first problem which comes up, lack of knowledge.

Lack of knowledge is a major hurdle for many people. It is very difficult to take advantage of benefits when you don't know about them. That should show you how I feel about the need for knowledge. It is crucial, but you need to be careful as to the knowledge you are receiving. Let me give you an example.

After I ask the question about deducting the educational expenses, my next question is: "Why not?" The response I get is important because it demonstrates the type of information being disseminated out there. I have many people who tell me that they didn't deduct this expense because their accountant told them that they couldn't take that deduction. Let me begin by saying that the accountant is right. *They* can't take that

deduction. The problem is that they didn't ask the right question. The accountant answered the question which was asked. Do you sometimes feel like you're getting the wrong answers out of life? Perhaps you're asking the wrong questions.

> *Do you sometimes feel like you're getting the wrong answers out of life? Perhaps you're asking the wrong questions.*

Asking the right questions falls under the category of knowledge. You need to know the right questions to ask if you are looking for the answers that you want. I want to show you how I experienced this.

When I was in law school, I had a course on federal income taxation. One day during class, I asked the law professor whether the expense of law school courses was deductible. The professor's response was that these expenses were not deductible. Actually, he went into great length to explain that there are few instances in the entire tax code as clear cut as the non-deductibility of these expenses.

I must admit that this is not the answer that I wanted to hear. But wait a second. I did get the correct answer to the question I asked. Fortunately, I recognized the problem and immediately asked a follow-up question.

This follow-up question relates to a question I ask at the seminars as I mentioned earlier. Basically, I was in the exact situation that my students find themselves in. I had asked a very well-respected tax expert an important question and I got the wrong answer. Not the wrong answer to the question, but the wrong answer from the one I was looking for.

Do you suppose that this could stop a person dead in their tracks? Sure. The key is that we must have enough knowledge to get to the next step.

At the seminars, after I hear about what the accountants have told the students, I ask a new question. The question is: "How many of you work for a corporation who will either reimburse you or pay for college courses which

you take?" All of a sudden, hands shoot up all over the class. I then ask those students whether they think that that corporation deducted that expense. Their answer is a resounding yes!

But wait a second, I thought that our accountant told us that we can't deduct that expense. I thought that my law professor said that these expenses are not deductible. How is it then that the corporation can deduct these expenses? What's the difference?

The difference is that those companies are corporations. As corporations, things work a little differently. Corporations can deduct things which individuals simply cannot. Why can't people take those deductions? Lack of entities.

That is the second hurdle which people must overcome. If you do not have a corporation, you cannot receive the benefits of corporations. Entities do you no good whatsoever if you don't have the entities.

The thing you need to understand is that there are two stumbling blocks which people are faced with out there. These are:

1.   Lack of knowledge, and
2.   Lack of entities.

One important point is that both of these must be mastered. If you have knowledge of entities, but you don't have the actual entities, what good does this do you? Conversely, if you have entities but don't have the knowledge to effectively use the entities, how much better off are you? In essence, one cannot work without the other.

The real issue is how to overcome these areas which we are lacking in. Which should be tackled first? That can be rather tricky but it needs to be addressed if we plan on achieving any sort of meaningful results.

Setting up entities is easy. Anyone can go out and find an attorney to set

up any type of entity that they want. It reminds me a little bit of the stock market. Is it difficult to purchase stock? No. Once you go out and purchase the stock, does that mean that you will automatically achieve the optimal results? Not at all. It works the same way with entities. You need to know what to do with it once you purchase it. You need the knowledge.

While knowledge alone will not make you successful, lack of knowledge can certainly make you unsuccessful.

Once you determine that you need the knowledge, where do you go to get it? Do colleges teach you how to actually implement strategies or do they teach theory? Remember that college course, How to Operate Legal Entities 101? It's not there is it? Do books really take you step-by-step through the actual day-to-day workings of your legal entities? To truly understand how to do these things, you need to learn it in a way where you can really *learn*.

It was with this thought in mind that I developed an intensive hands-on training program for operating your legal entities and actually implementing these strategies. It is the cream of the crop when it comes to interactive workshops.

We call it Secret Millionaire Mastery™. It is not truly a seminar, but more of a workshop. When I say workshop, I mean that you will be *working*. This is no lecture setting, but an actual interactive environment where people get things done. We show people how to make sense out of legal requirements and understand technical legal jargon. It is a literal buffet of knowledge.

The workshop is a course designed as a step-by-step process for accomplishing your wealth objectives through the proper use of your legal entities. Specifically, we go through how forms need to be filled out, the steps which need to be followed for taking advantage of strategies to help you protect your assets, plan your estate, and reduce your tax bill. We spend a great deal of time on how records need to be kept, not only the minutes of your formal meetings, but specific resolutions for documenting and implementing changes or policies within you legal entities. We spend a good deal of time walking you through the flow of money from one entity to another as well so that when you leave, you are well-equipped to operate as a Secret Millionaire. People will get more accomplished with their legal entities during their time at the Secret Millionaire Mastery™ workshop than they may have accomplished during any other period of their entire life.

The Secret Millionaire Mastery™ program is an event which is structured in a way to enable graduates to hit the ground running, fast. I'd love to be able to say that it is the best workshop of its kind, but in terms of effectiveness, it is the *only* workshop of its kind. It is an absolute learning revolution. You will gain a knowledge of the daily operation of your legal entities which will fully prepare you for more advanced strategy implementation of your legal entities.

The goal of this program is to provide a setting where people have the opportunity to make things happen. I learned a long time ago that you have two choices. You can either *wait* for things to happen, or you can go out and *make* things happen. Which type of person are you? You and you alone are in control over what type of person you are.

As I conclude this book, I'm excited. I'm excited about the opportunities available for you to go out and really make things happen. I'm excited about what you can do, not only for yourselves, but for your families. When all is said and done, you have a decision to make. You are the one responsible for what you do with what you've been presented. You can go on doing things the same old way which will produce the same old results. Or, you can do things the way millionaires do things. If you want to get different results, you must do things differently. You must become a Secret Millionaire!

> *If you want to get different results, you must do things differently. You must become a Secret Millionaire!*

APPENDIX I
SPECIAL PREVIEW OF ANOTHER BOOK BY THE AUTHOR

The following excerpt is from another book I wrote a while back which was designed to assist clients with maintaining essential records associated with protecting their assets, planning their estates and reducing their taxes. I believe that it is of special interest to anyone interested in installing an "asset security system" and as such, I have included it in this appendix to the book. For more information on this book or any of the educational materials and/or services related to this book, please call Profit Publishing Group, Inc. toll-free at 877.868.9742.

MILLIONHEIRS™

In many ways, this may well be one of the most important books you ever read. This is not so much for what you will learn from the contents but more from what you will accomplish through the use of this book. That's right, the *use* of this book. Let me explain what I mean by that.

This book is not designed for your reading pleasure. It is designed to help you in an area where people often find themselves in an utterly confused state. It is a planning guide, but it is also much more than that. It is a book about *your* life.

That may sound strange to you at first. Think about it. How on earth could I write a book about you when I don't even know you. The way I'm able to do this is that you will be an associate author. You may have never thought of yourself as an author but that is exactly what you will become as you use this book.

With that thought in mind, let's take a closer look at what this book is all about. In order for you to fully understand the purpose of this book, you need to understand how the book came about. Let me explain that to you.

One night, I was at a dinner party for some friends and I started talking to a friend of mine. The topic of that conversation was a topic I find myself talking about rather frequently, business. It just so happens that my friend is in a business very similar to mine and we had been thinking along similar lines about a new business idea. Through that conversation, the idea for this book was first developed.

To give you a little background, I am an attorney specializing in the areas of asset protection, estate planning, and tax reduction. In this area of specialization, I travel throughout the country speaking with people from all walks of life on how they can preserve more of the wealth that

they have spent their lives accumulating. Additionally, I spend a great deal of my time developing products outlining exactly how individuals can accomplish these important objectives. Along these lines, I had recently been thinking about developing a new product.

Now, I told you that my friend is in a similar business to mine. He is a certified public accountant (CPA) specializing in the area of taxation. In this concentration, he deals with small business owners and others who have created large amounts of wealth on a regular basis. With this background, he had identified an important need of these individuals and had been heavily involved in forming a business to address that need.

During our conversation, he told me that he was well into the process of developing that new business with a couple of our mutual friends. In outlining the concept behind their business, I realized that we were on the same page so to speak in our thinking. I told him a little bit about what I had been working toward and we came to an agreement. It was time to form an alliance.

This book is a product of that alliance. It is the first portion of a package designed to assist you immensely with an area of crucial significance to you and your loved ones. Specifically, this is a program which will provide for your family.

The idea behind this program is simple. The problem however, is that it is too often overlooked. In fact, you yourself may have overlooked this important area. To make that determination, you need to ask yourself a few simple questions.

If your father/mother passed away today, would you know how to take care of all of their affairs? If you think you can, take a closer look by asking yourself a few more questions. Would you know what credit cards they have in their name and how to cancel those credit cards? If not, you may find yourself in a situation where someone could obtain those card numbers and go out on a shopping spree.

Take a look at some of the following questions to see what type of situation you could find yourself in:

- Do you know whether or not they owe anyone any money? If they do, how much?
- Do you know whether or not anyone owes them any money? If so, how much?
- Are they involved in any business transactions or investments which owe them money?
- What types of bank accounts or brokerage accounts do they have and where are they?
- How much money is in each of these accounts? How do you know?
- Is there any money and/or other valuables hidden in a special area? If so, where is it?
- Is there anyone who needs to be contacted? If so, who? When?
- What type of estate planning do they have? Do they have any estate planning?
- What is involved in the handling of their estate?
- What type of financial situation are they in?
- Do they have money in retirement accounts? If so, where? How much?
- Do they have insurance? If so, how much? What type? Who is it with? Who are the beneficiaries of the policy?
- How much are the items in their estate worth?

Are you beginning to get the picture? Some of you reading this book may think that you know the answers to these questions. Let me ask you another important question, however. Are you sure?

You see, too many times people find themselves in a lost world when it comes to this issue. Estate planning is certainly about wills, trusts, insurance, and other instruments. But it is also about planning things which may seem quite simple and mundane, yet prove to be the most difficult of all.

When I first started thinking about this, I put myself to the test. I actually knew more about my parents' situation than most but it scared me to death to think about all of the horrible consequences which I might face without proper planning. Perhaps the most frightening thing is that the overwhelming vast majority of individuals will never do anything about it.

I started thinking about times when my parents told me to check through everything with a fine toothed comb before I got rid of it. I distinctly remember an instance when my father told me about one thousand dollars which was hidden in a secret compartment of his desk. What would happen if I forgot about this and sold the desk for $300? Someone would get a great deal that's for sure. It's also sure that it wouldn't be me.

You may be thinking that all you need to do is to sit down and talk about things and you will simply remember it all. Folks, you may have a good memory but memory alone is not a plan. Memories tend to fade. Besides that, your thinking doesn't tend to work as clearly when you find yourself in a situation where you've lost a loved one.

This book has been assembled in a way that will assist you tremendously when you find yourself in this type of situation. We have set forth specific areas of concern which will need to be addressed when that time comes. We have gone to great lengths to include all of those items which tend to be forgotten in those stressful times surrounding loss.

Let me assure you, this is no small undertaking. People often neglect to pay attention to some of the smallest, yet most important issues. That's where we come in. To give you a sense of what those items might entail, ask yourself the following questions:

*If your father/mother passed away today, would you know:
- where they would like to be buried?
- if they would like to be buried rather than other options?
- where they would like their funeral to be held?

- how they would like the funeral to be organized?
- who they would want to give the eulogy?
- what songs they would like as a part of the funeral?

The questions which must be answered go on and on. The sad reality is that people find themselves in a situation where they do not know how to handle things.

You may find yourself in a situation right now where your parents are already deceased. You may remember how difficult the process was when you went through it, but now it's over. You may feel that you have things covered. Now, however, I want you to think about something a little different. You know the confusion which accompanies the inability to answer the previous questions? How does that feel? Think about it.

Now I want you to think to yourself exactly how your family would handle things in the event that you were to pass away tomorrow. Would they be able to answer all of the questions I posed earlier? Have you left them properly equipped?

Chances are, you are in no better shape than the majority of those who fail to plan. Even though you've purchased the insurance, structured your will and/or trusts, you still haven't taken care of some of the most important details. The key now is to determine how to take control over the situation. The simple truth is, if you don't take control of the situation, the situation will take control of you.

Once you decide to gain control, it's time to take action. I mentioned earlier that this book is the first part of the overall program. Through the use of this book, you will equip yourself and your family with the tools needed to deal with things. The book will play a central role in getting you started in the right direction.

The next part of the program is to get assistance. I told you earlier about

my friend with whom I formed this powerful business alliance. His vision was to design a company which would take a lot of the headaches out of the process. The idea is to provide a service where records are kept for family members and many of the difficult tasks are handled in a way which enables the family more flexibility to deal with the issues surrounding this unfortunate time. That powerful idea came to life in the form of Vantage Planning LLC.

Through this business, families are able to provide detailed instructions for handling their affairs in those difficult times. Parents are able to structure things in a way which takes a great deal of stress out of the entire scenario. By using the service, parents are able to outline exactly how things should function. A brief description of the company and the services which they provide is included in the section entitled, "Additional Resources", located at the back of this book.

Everything included in this book and the services provided is designed with the idea of creating a plan for you and your family. Too many times, these plans are never designed. The problem is that people are always aiming to get around to it. People think that they will take care of things "later". In the real world, however, "later" can come much sooner than you realize.

No matter how much time you spend on becoming successful, you must make sure you avoid becoming a failure. What I mean by this is that you must have a plan. Because when all is said and done, *if you fail to plan, you plan to fail!*

APPENDIX II:

SECRET MILLIONAIRE RESOURCE MATERIALS

THE EDUCATIONAL MATERIALS AND PRODUCTS FEATURED IN THIS CATALOG ARE AVAILABLE THROUGH PROFIT PUBLISHING GROUP, INC. BY CALLING TOLL-FREE 1.877.868.9742 OR BY VISITING US ON THE WEB AT WWW.SECRETMILLIONAIRE.COM.

A personal note from J.J. Childers, attorney and author of *The Secret Millionaire Series:*

Dear Friend:

For the past several years I've been actively involved in educating thousands of people from all over this great country on how to effectively structure their financial affairs to deal with the important concerns of asset protection, estate planning and tax reduction. Through this endeavor, I've been fortunate to meet, learn from and work with some of the greatest financial and business minds in the nation. Profit Publishing Group, Inc., is the company I established to pass this knowledge on to you through my seminars and through the educational materials that are available at the seminars; but many of you have told met that this is simply not enough. With the hectic schedules of most Americans today (myself included!) you need the information to come to you at your convenience.

In response to this, I am extremely excited to present to you a brand new catalog of my most popular educational products. Until now these products have been available only through the seminars. Now you can study my different courses where ever, whenever and however many times you choose. You make the seminar schedule and you choose the order in which you take the courses. Study them in the peace and quiet of your home, on your commute to work, with your family or with your financial planner. You decide.

The key to building a secure financial plan for yourself and your family is to design the proper plan to fit your needs. Through my exciting product line, you can gain the necessary knowledge to accumulate and preserve vast amounts of wealth. I urge you to call today to get started protecting your assets, reducing taxes and planning your estate for the future. Don't allow yourself to be left out of the growing ranks of Secret Millionaires!

Sincerely,

J.J. Childers

Who is the Secret Millionaire? What does it mean to be a Secret Millionaire? How can I become a Secret Millionaire? The answer to these questions can make the difference between a life of wealth and abundance and a life of looking in from the outside.

Have you ever wondered what it is about one person who may not seem to be as talented as others, yet obtains results that others only dream about? Have you ever thought that there must be some sort of secret that certain people know about that you don't? Does it sometimes seem unfair that others less talented and knowledgeable than you somehow are in a better financial situation? The truth of the matter is that they DO know something that you don't. These individuals have mastered the art of being a Secret Millionaire.

If you would like to obtain the type of results that millions of people only dream about, then you must LEARN how to do it. As with anything in life, there is a definite process in becoming and being wealthy. Once you begin to implement that process into your life, you will begin to receive those things which you desire. You will become a Secret Millionaire.

But why become a "secret" millionaire? For most people, the idea of ever actually attaining millionaire status is something to be so proud of that they would shout it from the mountain tops. The problem with this is that that is when the vultures come. Do you suppose that your attractiveness to those wanting money goes up or down as you accumulate wealth? Of course it goes up, up, up. The most important characteristic of a Secret Millionaire is to keep their profile low thus warranting less attention and scrutiny. The bottom line is that your wealth is no one's business. In order to continually build your wealth you must master the art of conducting yourself as a Secret Millionaire.

The Secret Millionaire Mastery™ program is designed to help anyone who truly desires wealth to obtain it, and most importantly, keep it. Following time-tested and proven principles, gained through years of in-depth study and experience, the program will guide you through your journey to success.

Building on this foundation, The Secret Millionaire Mastery™ program takes you step by step through the process of creating, accumulating, and preserving wealth. The Secret Millionaire Mastery™ process is outlined and explained in detail on the following pages. Through disciplined and thorough implementation of these principles, untold wealth for you and your family is just a matter of time.

SECRET MILLIONAIRE
HOME STUDY COURSES & EDUCATIONAL MATERIALS

Developing specialized knowledge is absolutely essential to being successful. A major problem that often plagues people is that they gain this knowledge and then fail to effectively utilize it. As we all know, once you acquire certain skills, those skills can be lost or fade over time if not periodically practiced and updated. Our home study courses and educational materials can help you to increase your basic knowledge of the material or, most importantly, for continued learning. You must continue to learn. We live in a world of ever-increasing change requiring continued learning just to keep up, let alone getting ahead.

Through continuing to learn and study the Secret Millionaire process, you have the opportunity to continually build upon the base level foundation of knowledge. The great thing about these materials is that the information is placed into a medium which makes it easy to review over and over again enabling you to not only reaffirm your understanding but to solidify it as well. Do you suppose that you would gain more from hearing the same thing the second time than you did the first? Of course you would. The wonderful part of this series is that you have the information at your fingertips and can take full advantage of the wealth of knowledge contained therein.

Because the entire Secret Millionaire series is set forth in an educational format, the supplemental educational materials are designed to take you from one step to the next without leaving you confused. By beginning with introductory material before moving on to the more advanced concepts, the program enables anyone to master the art of wealth if they simply take the time to learn how to do it.

SECRET MILLIONAIRE RESOURCE MATERIALS

The Secret Millionaire resource materials are broken down into various components as follows: 1) Audio/Video Tape Sets with complimentary CD's 2) The Secret Millionaire book series 3) The Secret Millionaire Monthly Newsletter 4) The Secret Millionaire website and 5) The Secret Millionaire computer software. These diverse products are offered, because we know that in order to truly gain a thorough understanding of such a dynamic subject, it is best to completely immerse yourself into all aspects and mediums. Remember, it is an absolute law of nature that *you become what you think about*. For this reason, the Secret Millionaire series provides the necessary tools for you to make the wealth wisdom and millionaire mentality part of your everyday life and to continue to grow in your wealth knowledge.

THE SECRET MILLIONAIRE AUDIO/VIDEO TAPE SERIES™

THE SECRET MILLIONAIRE
WEALTH FORTRESS™

The Secret Millionaire Wealth Fortress™gives you the answers to the who, what, where, when, why, and how questions teaching you how you too can implement the various wealth tools of the affluent. This multi-media system is designed to complement and enhance your live seminar experience. Special emphasis is placed on the mechanics of the various entities including much needed information on how to actually conduct your business and everyday affairs through the use of legal entities.

THE AUDIO PRESENTATION: Relive the power and energy of The Secret Millionaire™ Seminars by owning The Secret Millionaire Wealth Fortress™ audio tape set. Increase your wealth knowledge by "attending" these audio courses again and again at your convenience. Share the valuable knowledge and information contained in this audio workshop with your family, friends and financial advisors.

VIDEO PRESENTATION SERIES: One of the best ways to gain a better understanding of something is to see it. You need to visualize the fact that operating your own financial empire is more than just a bunch of paperwork and legal jargon, it is a way of life. In this exciting video presentation series, attorney and author J.J. Childers not only explains these strategies, he shows you some of the incredible ways that you can implement amazing wealth techniques into your own situation. Through the interview format of the videos, you are able to gain a greater insight into the world of wealth by having difficult legal and tax issues explained in no-nonsense terms. You will not want to miss a single minute of this high-impact wealth strategy information.

Audio and video workshops are included for each of the following entities: 1) Corporations; 2) Limited Partnerships; 3) Limited Liability Companies; 4) Trusts; and 5) Retirement Plans. A sampling of the high-powered information contained in this series is as follows:
• Using entities to minimize risk/maximize cash flow • Start entities with no minimum capital • Get your entities running ASAP • How and why you turn your sole proprietorship into a corporation • Understanding and using different classes of stock • How to operate a limited partnership for business or investments • How your entities can reduce your taxable income • Move your existing assets into legal entities • Retirement entities overview • Maintaining control of your pension funds • Why your retirement plan should be self-trusteed • Using a living trust to avoid probate • What is the trust relationship • How a trust can provide continuity for your assets • Reduce, or even eliminate your estate taxes• Integrating the corporation with other entities • Lowering your tax bracket through your entities • How millionaires can have a taxable estate near zero • and this is just a sampling of the valuable information contained in these cassettes!   WFAV101

More in-depth descriptions of the audio workshop titleswhich are included in The Wealth Fortress™ are on the following pages:

SECRET MILLIONAIRE MASTERY™

The knowledge and expertise shared at The Secret Millionaire Mastery™ live seminar can be studied and shared interminably when you have the supplemental audio workshop at your command. This pinnacle of the Secret Millionaire series is a culmination of the wealth principles taught in the other exceptional wealth training courses. The sheer volume of information and knowledge studied in the Secret Millionaire Mastery™ course makes this take home version a "must have" tool for your wealth toolchest. Make certain that you have a copy of the crown jewel of specialized knowledge.

THE CORPORATE CONFERENCE™

The Secret Millionaire's Corporate Conference™ is the definitive course on the cornerstone of the overall entity-structuring plan. In this sensational audio workshop, you will see how you can begin operating your own corporation to attain the level of success you are aiming for. This is where you will learn exactly what it is that you can achieve through the use of one of the  oldest business machines. Through this course, you will gain access to the closely-guarded secrets of today's multi-national companies on how the big boys do business. Now it's your turn to take advantage of these powerful strategies.

THE LIMITED PARTNERSHIP PROGRAM™

The limited partnership is an often used but seldom explained entity that can transform your business and investments into a virtual money engine for accumulating wealth. In this exceptional educational experience, you will learn fabulous strategies for planning your estate, protecting your assets and significantly reducing your taxes. Through a plethora of illustrations and examples you will learn how to divide assets amongst yourself and family members to gain the advantages of a wealth tool used by many of the country's most affluent families. Special emphasis is given on the role of the limited partnership in the overall wealth plan and its effectiveness as an entity enhancement tool when combined with other legal entities. This audio course is especially important for anyone concerned about leaving more of their estate to the government than to their beneficiaries.

LIMITED LIABILITY COMPANY COMPOSIUM™

The limited liability company has taken the business world by storm as the hottest new tool for accomplishing the all-important goals of protecting assets and reducing taxes. As more and more businesses and business people continue to form this impressive new entity, the need to be fully informed on its use becomes greater and greater. In this highly valuable audio program, you will learn the ins and outs of the limited liability company seeing how it can be used by you and your business to achieve the type of results that you are looking for. Do not allow yourself to miss out on the exceptional information contained in this phenomenal educational experience.

SECRET MILLIONAIRE TRUST TRAINING™

No legal entity is more synonymous with wealth than the trust. Trusts and trust funds are often made reference to yet the vast majority of people have no idea whatsoever as to what a trust is. In this exclusive audio journey into the world of trusts, you will learn exactly what a trust is as well as what it is not. You will gain valuable insight into how and why trusts are used by the wealthiest families in this country. Most importantly, you will learn how you can begin to take advantage of the closely-guarded wealth secrets and strategies available through trusts. Special attention will be given to the different types of trusts, the various uses of trusts, and the day to day functions of trusts and how they can help you to accomplish the necessary objectives for creating, accumulating and preserving wealth. The Secret Millionaire Trust Training™ is the sine qua non to understanding the ways of the wealthy.

SECRET MILLIONAIRE RETIREMENT PLANNING WORKSHOP™

Turn your ordinary retirement plan into an extraordinary tool for wealth by gaining highly sought after pension and retirement plan secrets in this dynamic workshop. While the subject of retirement plans is not typically an area that generates a lot of excitement, the powerful strategies that you will learn in this program will leave you exhilarated. Whether you are interested in establishing a pension, IRA, or other type of retirement plan, or are simply looking for a way to turbo-charge your current plan, you will want to seize the opportunities presented in this audio course. This is an absolute must for anyone looking to build wealth in one of the safest and most protected asset accounts available.

Other audio titles available in the Secret Millionaire™ series include:

SECRET MILLIONAIRE ASSET PROTECTION WORKSHOP™

This dynamic new advanced asset protection audio training focuses on an area of immense importance in today's litigious society, asset protection. Leading experts in the field of asset protection will be presenting some of the latest and greatest strategies and tactics for protecting and shielding your family's financial holdings from the ever-increasing dangers prevalent in today's hostile legal environment. Now more than ever, you must do what it takes to learn the important techniques for safeguarding your family's financial future. APAV108

SECRET MILLIONAIRE ESTATE PLANNING WORKSHOP™

In this exciting new offering, you will learn exactly what you MUST do in order to preserve your family's hard-earned assets from the devastating effects of taxes, fees, and other asset destroyers upon death. The key to avoiding these and other traumatic events is to implement a sound financial and estate plan for yourself and your family. In this audio training program you will learn advanced strategies designed solely for designing a customized estate plan. You must learn how to structure that plan. EPAV109

SECRET MILLIONAIRE TAXATION TRAINING™

The dreaded issue of taxes is the focus of this training. Specifically, avoiding as many taxes as possible is the primary thrust of the Secret Millionaire Taxation Training. This advanced training

is designed to delve deeper into the important topic of your taxes and answer your important questions. What can you deduct? What can you not deduct? How can you avoid an audit? What are the little-known secrets to taking as much in deductions as the law allows? The answers to these and other questions will enable you to put dollars in your pocket through tax savings. If you'd like to pay less in taxes, get to this training! TXAV110

SECRET MILLIONAIRE STOCK TRADER STRUCTURING WORKSHOP™

Are you trading in the stock market? If you are, chances are that you're doing so successfully or you'd no longer be doing it. If that's the case, you are in a situation where you must learn to effectively manage capital gains. The taxes involved in stock trading oftentimes wipe portfolios out. But there's much more than just taxes involved. What are you doing about the areas of estate planning and asset protection? Traders must learn the proper way to structure their trading "business" in order to keep more of what they earn. The Secret Millionaire Stock Trader Structuring Workshop will teach you how to do it. STAV111

SECRET MILLIONAIRE REAL ESTATE INVESTOR STRUCTURING WORKSHOP™

Real estate investors and developers face issues which are different from those faced by most people. The risk of lawsuits is incredible, not to mention the tax issues associated with owning and maintaining real estate. Would you be interested in learning how to structure your real estate

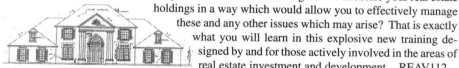

holdings in a way which would allow you to effectively manage these and any other issues which may arise? That is exactly what you will learn in this explosive new training designed by and for those actively involved in the areas of real estate investment and development. REAV112

SECRET MILLIONAIRE SMALL BUSINESS STRUCTURING WORKSHOP™

Small business owners are the wheels that keep this country rolling. Anyone who is involved in owning and operating their own small business is well aware of the fact that there are advantages and disadvantages. In this high-powered workshop, you will learn exciting ways of structuring your business and personal financial affairs in a way which can enable you to maximize the advantages and minimize any perceived disadvantages. The tax code is packed full of potential deductions for the small businessperson. The key is to learn how to take these deductions. Doing so means more money for you and your families! SBAV113

THE SECRET
MILLIONAIRE

ADDITIONAL SECRET MILLIONAIRE™ EDUCATIONAL MATERIALS

THE SECRET MILLIONAIRE MONTHLY™ NEWSLETTER

Your subscription will bring you one full year of the definitive monthly guide to current trends and laws regarding increasing and securing your assets. This publication includes excerpts from the exclusive Secret Millionaire Graduate Series™, as well as timely, up-to-the-minute information on legal decisions that could have an effect on you, ways to reduce your tax burden, planning your estate for your heirs, protecting and keeping more of your hard-earned assets, consumer tips on popular goods, upcoming product releases, seminar schedules, frequently asked questions and more, delivered right to you. This monthly publication is written by experts in their fields and presented in an attractive, easy-to-read format that provides you with the tools and information you need to keep on top of breaking issues. SMNW201

www.secretmillionaire.com

Now available on the world wide web, www.secretmillionaire.com provides a perfect introduction to the Secret Millionaire philosophy, products and services. In addition to our on-line catalog and ordering, secretmillionaire.com offers an inside look into the company and the man behind The Secret Millionaire, as well as weekly updated tips, upcoming product launches, seminar schedules and links to other recommended sites.

THE SECRET MILLIONAIRE™ BOOKS

As university and college courses have textbooks to supplement students' learning and retention, The Secret Millionaire Mastery™ presents The Secret Millionaire™ book series. These books are packed with the same information that can be found in the Secret Millionaire™ seminars and audio and video tape sets and serve as an essential reference tool for honing your skills and implementing your mastery plan. New titles are being continually developed, so call for recent and upcoming releases.

THE SECRET MILLIONAIRE™ SOFTWARE

Use your personal computer to organize your assets and educate yourself and your family about the principles of the Secret Millionaire Mastery program. Call for new software program availability.

SECRET MILLIONAIRE
SPECIALIZED TRAINING SERIES

Once you have begun to think like a Secret Millionaire, the next step is to become proficient in the strategies utilized by the Secret Millionaire. You must work to obtain the necessary knowledge to become wealthy. More than simply acquiring knowledge, you must acquire what is referred to as specialized knowledge. It is this specialized knowledge which will set you apart from the masses and propel you into the ranks of the super-wealthy.

But what is meant by the term "specialized knowledge"? Do you suppose that the wealthy are privy to certain secrets which are not readily available to everyone? The answer to this is both yes and no. While the  wealthy are indeed privy to certain wealth secrets, these secrets are readily available to all those who are willing to do what it takes to obtain them. When it comes to specialized knowledge, the wealthy realize that you must learn the secrets of success. Part of the secret is to gain certain skills. Through the Secret Millionaire Strategy Training courses, you can develop a deep understanding of the strategies and tactics used to create, accumulate, and preserve vast amounts of wealth for you and your family.

Below and on the following page is a detailed listing and description of the specific live seminar courses available for obtaining your wisdom of wealth.

SECRET MILLIONAIRE
STRATEGY TRAINING COURSES

THE SECRET MILLIONAIRE WEALTH STRUCTURING WORKSHOP™

What would it be like to sit in on a high-powered strategy session with a Secret Million-aire? The best way to find out is to actually do it. In this dynamic presentation on Secret Millionaire strategies, you will learn not only the basics of wealth tools, but how they can be combined one with another for maximum profit, savings and effectiveness. You will learn how you too can implement the wealth enhancement tactics utilized by some of today's most savvy profes-sionals. This course is designed as the basis upon which all other courses are built upon. Here you will gain the initial wealth knowledge to enable you to best determine your course of action for the future of your finances. It is crucial that you get a handle on the various tools available for accomplishing key financial objectives and the Secret Millionaire Wealth Structuring Workshop™ is the place to do it. It is an absolute must for anyone serious about gaining the general knowledge necessary for obtaining wealth. WSWSM401

THE CORPORATE CONFERENCE™

The Secret Millionaire's Corporate Conference™ is the definitive course on the cornerstone of the overall entity-structuring plan. In this sensational program, you will see how you can begin operating your own corporation to attain the level of success you are aiming for. This is where you will learn exactly what it is that you can achieve through the use of one of the oldest business machines. Through this course, you will gain access to the closely-guarded secrets of today's multi-national companies on how the big boys do business. Now it's your turn to take advantage of these powerful strategies. CCSM402

SECRET MILLIONAIRE ADVANCED WEALTH TRAINING™

Secret Millionaire Advanced Wealth Training™ is the pinnacle of the Secret Millionaire training series. Just as in colleges and universities across the world, prerequisites are required for attending the upper level courses such as this one. The caliber of information covered in this two-day event is targeted only for those who have acquired and demonstrated a base level foundation of knowledge upon which to build. That knowledge must be obtained prior to attending this prestigious gathering as it is a culmination of the wealth principles taught in the other exceptional wealth training courses. Building on the information covered throughout the Secret Millionaire series, the Secret Millionaire Mastery™ course takes it to the next level by offering sophisticated wealth creation, accumulation and preservation strategies otherwise unavailable to the public. The information covered in this setting is exclusively for those who qualify based on the criteria established by the Secret Millionaire Board of Advisors. It is the crowning point of Secret Millionaire specialized knowledge. MSSM403

SECRET MILLIONAIRE OFFSHORE MASTERY™

No longer an exclusive haven for the ultrawealthy, offshore entities are prime investment options for thousands of Americans like yourself. Learn how modern technology allows you to keep on top of the global marketplace and handle your investments like never before! In addition to guiding you through often lucrative and volatile international investing opportunities, the ultimate in privacy and asset protection can be achieved through the establishment of offshore entities. Learn from experts how to establish, structure and operate your offshore entities to maximize privacy, protection and accesibility to your hard-earned assets. OSSM404

CALL 1.877.868.9742 TO PLACE AN ORDER, OR FOR PRICING OR ADDITIONAL INFORMATION

THE SECRET MILLIONAIRE
MASTER MIND GROUP

Perhaps the most vital part of any overall success plan is assembling your team. While many people feel that they must rely upon themselves rather than others, there is a fine line between balancing this dichotomy. It is indeed true that you simply cannot rely upon others to do things for you. However, when you work as part of what is known as a "master mind" team, your capabilities, potential and productivity are compounded. For example, when Henry Ford set out to create the first V-8 engine, do you suppose he tried to do it all himself? Of course not. He assembled a team of the world's most brilliant minds, including Thomas Edison himself. By doing this, he was thus able to accomplish far more than any one team member could have ever accomplished on their own, regardless of their brilliance.

> *...the most vital part of any overall success plan is assembling your team.*

This element of the Secret Millionaire program takes this concept and applies this power to the process of creating, accumulating and preserving wealth. Through the offering of unique and sophisticated professional services, you reap the benefits of years of knowledge and experience enabling you to catapult several leaps forward on your journey to riches. By assembling a team of some of the country's brightest financial and legal minds to provide the essential services for obtaining and conserving wealth, the Secret Millionaire program empowers you to utilize the greatest tool of the world's wealthy, the "master mind" team.

> *...utilize the greatest tool of the world's wealthy, the "mastermind" team.*

The various services available through the Secret Millionaire program are divided by category so that you can gain access to the experts in each particular field based on your needs. A brief description of the categories along with a sampling of the services provided is listed on the following pages for your convenience. All of our services are custom tailored to suit your situation so there's no need to worry that you are missing a necessary element in your team or paying for canned services that you don't need. Your mastermind team is the quintessential ingredient in achieving your financial goals. By taking advantage of the Secret Millionaire Master Mind Group, the magic of the "master mind" is right at your fingertips.

CORPORATE SERVICES

The cornerstone of any good plan for wealth is the corporation. The opportunities available for accomplishing your financial objectives are abundant when the corporation is implemented properly. To make sure that things are indeed done properly, a wide array of services related to the corporation are available for you. A brief listing of the corporate services offered are:

•Turn-key Corporate Establishment services•Nominee Bank account set-up •Federal tax identification number •Resident agent services •Corporate office packages •Nominee officers and directors •Shelf (Aged) corporations •Corporate financial and tax consulting •Merchant account services •Establish corporate presence •Discreet brokerage account establishment •Nominee federal tax identification number for maximum privacy•   CPSV501

ENTITY ESTABLISHMENT SERVICES

Actually establishing the entities which become your tools of wealth is the first step in the process. Making sure that the entities are properly crafted is crucial. Through our entity establishment services, both of these concerns are taken care of. We offer a full-service program through which we establish these legal entities per your request. The legal entities which we will happily assemble for you include corporations, limited partnerships, limited liability companies, revocable living trusts, irrevocable life insurance trusts, and a variety of retirement planning options. Begin the process of creating your wealth today. EPSV502

RETIREMENT PLANNING

Planning for retirement involves much more than mapping out the destinations you wish to go. The most important part is to ensure that you have the necessary funds to travel, and to travel in style. Through our wide assortment of retirement planning tools, we can assist you in determining your retirement needs as well as assisting you with using you retirement plans for areas outside the realm of retirement including asset protection, estate planning and tax reduction for future generations. RPSV503

TRUST SERVICES

When utilizing these tools of the affluent, it becomes essential that you utilize a team of professionals who fully understand these tools. As you begin to create large amounts of wealth, the need increases to implement the tools which can best conserve that wealth. If what you are looking for is a group who understands the needs of the wealthy, our services are exactly what you've been searching for. Prompt, efficient service is what you will get when trying to make sense out of these sophisticated estate strategies. Our job is to keep you wealthy. TRSU504

TAX ADVISORY AND CONSULTATION

An unpleasant fact of life is that we have these things called "taxes". Of course, it takes these tax dollars to make things run smoothly so we all want to pay our fair share. If you believe that your "fair share" should be as next to nothing as possible, then you absolutely must take advantage of our tax advisory and consultation services. The nation's premier tax advisory specialists will assist you with making sense out of an area that can often seem like nonsense. TXAD505

TAX PREPARATION SERVICES

Another necessary evil is the filing of tax returns. As the tax law "evolves", we continually see more and more paperwork from the behemoth Internal Revenue Service. In order to assist you with this government bureaucracy, we offer a tax preparation service which is second to none. Our focus is on taking the worry out of income taxes so that your focus can be on those things which create more wealth. TXPR506

MILLIONHEIR™ MAINTENANCE

Million Heir™ Maintenance—The experts at Vantage Planning LLC, provide professional maintenance of your vital information along with the peace of mind which comes with knowing that your private records will be safeguarded for you and your loved ones. MHSV507

Call for specific pricing and services

OR VISIT OUR WEBSITE AT WWW.SECRETMILLIONAIRE.COM FOR ONLINE ORDERING AND UPDATES

Appendix III
Glossary of
Asset Security System Terminology

For more information on the terms listed in this glossary and the strategies with which they are associated, please call Profit Publishing Group, Inc. toll-free at 877.868.9742.

Accumulated earnings tax—A penalty tax charged against a corporation that retains an excessive amount of profits beyond the reasonable needs of its business, rather than distributing those profits to its owners. An LLC that is taxed as a partnership will not face this problem.

Adjusted gross income—All your income from whatever source (wages, rents, dividends, profits from a business, and so forth) less certain deductions (trade or business expenses, depreciation on rental property, allowable losses from sales of property, alimony payments, and so forth). Adjusted gross income, (sometimes called AGI) is important for calculating the amount of medical expenses and casualty losses that you can deduct. A modified version of adjusted gross income is used in determining how much Social Security is taxed. The $25,000 special allowance to deduct rental expenses when you actively participate is based on modified adjusted gross income, which is adjusted gross income increased by any passive activity losses, certain Social Security payments, and individual retirement account (IRA) deduction. This is important in assessing the value to an investment in the low-income housing credit.

Administrator—Person appointed by a court to administer and settle the estate of a person dying without a will, or the estate of a person who has a will but the appointed executor cannot serve; also called a personal representative.

Alternative minimum tax (AMT)—A second parallel tax system that many wealthier tax payers will have to consider when calculating their tax. The alternative minimum tax (or AMT) is calculated by starting with your taxable income calculated according to the regular tax rules. Add certain tax preference items and adjustments required by the AMT. Only certain itemized deductions are allowed. Next, subtract an exemption amount. The result is multiplied by either a 26 or 28 percent rate for individuals. If the tax due exceeds the tax you owe under the regular tax system then you must pay the larger alternative minimum tax.

Assets—Anything owned with monetary value. This includes both real and personal property.

Asset protection—The process of taking steps to minimize the risk of creditors or other claimants being able to reach your assets. This can include setting up a different entity, such as an LLC, for each property or business. Thus, if one particular property is subject to a suit (e.g., a tenant is hurt on one rental property), the claimant will be limited tot he assets from that particular property or entity. This can prevent a domino effect against your other assets. An LLC, just like a limited partnership, offers important benefits in the area of asset protection.

Attorney-in-fact—An agent who is given written authorization by you to take certain actions on your behalf.

Basis—Taxpayer's investment for tax purposes.

Beneficiary—A person for whom a trust is managed and who eventually receives the trust corpus after the death of the trust grantor. In another context, the beneficiary is the recipient of life insurance proceeds, benefit plans or gifts in a will.

Bequest—Property transferred under your will.

Calendar year—The accounting year beginning January 1 and ending December 31.

Capital expenditure—A payment to buy, build or improve an asset (property you own) that will last for more than one year. Capital expenditures generally can't be deducted in the year paid. Instead, they must usually be added to your investment (adjusted basis) in the asset and then be written off (depreciated) over a period of time.

Capital gain—The gain from selling a capital asset. The gain usually equals the amount realized or sales price less your investment (adjusted tax basis) in the property. Capital gains receive favorable tax treatment in that the maximum rate is set at 28 percent while the maximum tax rate on ordinary income is 39.6 percent. Capital losses can only be deducted in any year up to the amount of capital gains plus $3,000.

Capitalize—To add expenses that are not deductible to a person's investment (adjusted basis) in a property.

C Corporation—A regular corporation that pays federal taxes on its net income. A C corporation can be contrasted with and S corporation, which generally does not pay corporate level taxes; instead, its shareholders (owners) pay tax on their pro rata share of the S corporation's income.

Centralized management—One of four characteristics that distinguish an entity taxed as a partnership (flow-through income and loss to the owner) and an association taxable as a corporation (the corporate entity pays tax and then the owner pays tax on distributions received—called "double taxation"). Centralized management is a corporate (not partnership) characteristic.

Certificate or Articles of Incorporation—The document that creates a corporation according to the laws of the state. This must be filed with and approved by the state.

Charging order—A statutorily created means for a creditor of a judgment debtor who is a partner of others to reach the debtor's beneficial interest in the partnership, without risking dissolution of the partnership.

Charitable Remainder Trust (CRT)—The donation of property or money to a charity when the donor reserves the right to use the property or receive income from it for a specified number of years (or for life, or for the duration of the life of a second person such as a spouse). When the agreed period is over, the property belongs to the charitable organization.

Closely held business—A family business or business owned by relatively few individuals.

Codicil—An amendment to a will. The requirements for execution of a codicil are the same as for execution of a will. Therefore, if you are planning to make extensive changes to your will, it would generally be better to execute a new will rather than to amend an old will with codicils.

Continuity of life—One of the four characteristics that distinguish an entity taxed as a partnership and an association taxable as a corporation.

Contribution—Property transferred to an LLC in exchange for a membership interest in the LLC. This type of transfer is often referred to as a contribution of property to the LLC. Special tax rules will affect this transfer. Generally, you will not have a taxable gain on the contribution of property to an LLC in exchange for a membership interest.

Corporation—A business formed and authorized by law to act as a single entity, although it may be owned by one or more persons (called shareholders). It is legally endowed with rights and responsibilities and has a life of its own independent of the owners and operators. The owners are not personally liable for debts or obligations of the corporation. Corporations can be S corporations and C corporations.

Decedent—Person who has died. A decedent's assets are disposed of by will, or if no will exists by the intestacy laws of the decedent's state.

Deferral of estate tax—A provision of estate tax law. Where a sufficient portion of your estate comprises assets in a closely held and active business, your estate may qualify to pay the estate tax attributable to these assets over approximately a 14-year period instead of within nine months of death. The fact that a business interest is owned by an entity will not necessarily disqualify it for this favorable estate tax provision.

Deferral of income—A common tax planning technique near December 31. By not recognizing income until the next year, the taxpayer may postpone payment on the income for another full year. Examples of income deferral include delaying the sale of stocks or property until January, selling property on the installment method and not receiving cash until the next year, and so forth.

Depreciation—The writing off of an asset's cost over its useful life or using methods prescribed by the tax laws. Depreciation is based on the idea that property wears down over time from exposure to the elements, physical wear and tear from use, and so forth. Depreciation of assets held by your LLC or partnership will be passed to your personal tax return and deducted there as a part of the results you realize in that given tax year from your LLC or partnership.

Descendant—A person who is a relative in a direct line from another person, also called issue.

Discount—A discount on the value of a gift of a minority (less than controlling) and/or lack of marketability interest in an LLC may sometimes be claimed. This can enable the donor to give a greater percentage interest in the LLC as a gift in any year under the $10,000 annual exclusion without, for example, using any of the donor's unified credit.

Dissolution—Formal statutory liquidation, termination and winding up of a business entity.

Distribution—The parceling out of profits or other assets to members/owners of a legal entity. As a member/owner, you may receive distributions of cash or even property. Depending on the entity however, your tax results may not be limited to the amount you receive as a distribution. In a pass-thru taxation entity, you will be taxed on your pro rata portion of LLC income or loss.

Distributive share—The share of property inherited by a beneficiary when a decedent has died without a will. For example, a person dies with no surviving spouse and two surviving children, in most states, the children divide the estate equally. This would be each child's distributive share.

Double taxation—Occurs when corporations pay tax on corporate profits and share-holders pay income tax on dividend or distributive income.

Donee—A person who receives a gift.

Donor—A person who makes a gift.

Durable power of attorney—A document in which you grant certain people (your attorneys-in-fact) the authority to handle your financial matters, which will remain valid even if you become disabled. A plain (not durable) power of attorney will not be valid in that event.

Election—In accounting, the choice of a particular method for calculating taxes. The tax laws provide for optional treatment of many different items. Often the taxpayer must make an election (usually by filing a statement or checking a box on the tax return) as to which optional method will be used. Legal entities, as separate tax reporting entities, must make their own tax elections.

Employer Identification Number (EIN)—A number issued by state and federal governments to identify a business for tax purposes. In a sole proprietorship, your Social Security Number serves as your EIN.

Estate tax—A tax that may be due on the death of a taxpayer, as a result of the transfer of wealth to family and others. Exclusions are provided for transfers to the taxpayer's spouse, charities, and so forth. The tax rate for the estate tax can reach as high as 55 percent. A once-in-a-lifetime credit is permitted that enables you to pass property worth up to $600,000 to tohers (not including spouses) without having to pay a Federal estate tax.

Estimated tax—Income taxes paid by certain individuals on a quarterly basis to avoid underpayment penalties. Your expected income (or loss) from your investments must be considered in making these calculations.

Executor—An individual or institution named in a will to administer the estate of the person making the will. The executor legally steps into the shoes of the decedent and represents the estate in probate court. In some states the executor is also called the personal representative.

Fair market value—The price at which an item can be sold at the present time between tow unrelated people, neither under compulsion to buy or sell. Where a gift is made of an interest in an entity, it must be valued at its fair market value. This may, in the case of an LLC, be permitted to reflect a minority (lack of control) and/or lack of marketability discount.

Family limited partnership, or FLPs—A limited partnership owned by a family for purposes of transferring some of the value of the business or real estate to the younger generation and possibly involving them in the management of the business as well.

Fiduciary—A person having the legal duty to act primarily for the benefit of the principal. The fiduciary must act in the strictest confidence and trust. A trustee or an agent would be a fiduciary acting in behalf of the principal.

50-50 rule—A rule governing estate taxation of jointly held property between husband and wife. Under   this rule, only half the value of property owned by tenancies by the entirety or joint tenancies with rights of survivorship will be included in the gross estate of the first spouse to die, no matter how much or how little either spouse contributed. This is called the "50-50" rule.

Fiscal year—A tax year (12 month period) other than the calendar year used by a particular taxpayer. Some entities, such as LLCs and LPs are subject to limitations on when they can use a tax year other than the calendar year.

Foreign partnership—A partnership formed in one state or country but conducting some or all of its business in another state or country.

Formal will—A typed or printed will which must be witnessed and acknowledged by the testator to the effect that he is executing his or her will.

Free transferability—The ability to transfer ownership interest without the consent of other owners. A key characteristic in distinguishing the taxation of an LLC as a partnership or as an association taxable as a corporation. Where interests in your LLC can be freely transferred without restriction, it is more like a corporation than a partnership. The LLC's Operating Agreement could include restrictions so that, for example, the Manager, or 75 percent of the Members, may have to approve a transfer. Also, where the transfer is not approved, the person acquiring the interest is merely a substitute assignee and not an actual Member. Thus, certain important attributes of ownership may not be passed where the approval process is not obtained.

General partner—An owner of a partnership who is personally liable for all partnership debts and may be permitted to participate in the management of the partnership. Every limited partnership must have at least one general partner. Often this general partners is a corporation to avoid any one individual being personally liable.

General partnership—A partnership that has only general, no limited partners. This is the most common way for a few friends or investors to put their money together to buy a rental property or simple business. All partners share equally in contributions, distributions, and responsibilities. The risk here is that in a general partnership all partners are personally liable, without limit, for all partnership debts.

Generation-skipping transfer (GST) tax—A transfer tax generally assessed on transfers to grandchildren, great-grandchildren, and so on.

Gift—For purposes of taxation, the transfer of property without the donor receiving something of equal value in return. The federal government will assess a transfer tax where the value of the gift exceeds the $10,000 annual exclusion and your $600,000 unified credit equivalent is exhausted.

Gift splitting—A married couple's agreement to treat a gift made by one of them to a third party as having been made one-half by each. This lowers the gift tax rate and in many cases, significantly reduces, or even eliminates, any gift tax.

Gift tax—A tax that may be due when you give property or other assets away. You are allowed to give away a maximum of $10,000 per person (to any number of people) in any year without the tax applying. Above the $10,000 amount, you have a once-in-a-lifetime exclusion that permits your to give away $600,000 of property to any individuals other than a spouse without paying any gift tax. The gift tax and the estate tax are coordinate (unified) so that the $600,000 exclusion is only available once between them.

Grantor—The person who establishes a trust and transfers assets to it, also called a trustor or settlor.

Gross estate—The total value of the assets you own at death (less liabilities), or that are included in your estate. The value is determined at the date of your death or as of the alternate valuation date, which is six months following the date of death.

Gross income—All your earnings from all sources including wages, rents, royalties, dividends, interest, and so forth.

Gross value—The value of an estate before debts or encumbrances are paid. Probate fees are generally calculated on the gross value of the estate. For instance, if your estate consists of your residence with a market value of $200,000 and a mortgage of $125,000, probate fees would be based on the gross value of your estate which in this case would be $200,000.

Guardian—Someone who is legally responsible for the care and well-being of another person. A guardian is generally nominated in the case of a minor or when a person becomes disabled or incompetent. Guardians generally act under the supervision of a probate court and are responsible for all their actions to the court.

Heirs—The persons who receive your assets following your death.

Holographic will—This is a will entirely written, dated, and signed by the person in his or her own handwriting. I is permitted only in a few states, often under very limited circumstances.

Improvements—Payments for additions or betterments to property that will last more than a year and must thus be added to your investment (capitalized as part of your basis) in the property.

Incapacitated or incompetent—Someone who is unable to manage his or her own affairs either due to physical or mental impairment. An incompetent person cannot enter into a contract nor can he set up a trust, or appoint an agent to act on his behalf. In the absence of any suitable planning for disability, a court will have to be petitioned for the appointment of a guardian.

Inheritance tax—A tax on the right to receive property from a deceased person. Inheritance tax is measured by the share passing to each beneficiary.

Insolvency—When business liabilities exceed assets.

Installment sale—A sale where taxable gain is recognized over a number of years as payment is received for the property sold. If you are a dealer in property, you can't use the installment method. If you are a dealer in real estate, for example, but have a single property held as an investment, segregating that different property in an LLC may help support your position with the IRS that the particular property is different from those in which you are a dealer.

Insurance trust—An irrevocable trust established to own your insurance policies and thereby prevent them from being included in your estate. Insurance trusts are often used in planning for the tax interest in closely held businesses and nonliquid assets such as real estate.

Intangible assets or property—Property that you hold that has no intrinsic value but merely represents the value of underlying assets. Stocks and bonds are examples of this.

Interest—Entitlement to or being a permissible recipient of either the income or principal in a legal entity or asset. A reference to your ownership of a portion of an LLC. Also known as Membership Interest.

Intestate—Having died without a valid will. A person who dies with a will but fails to dispose of all his property is referred to as having left property by intestacy.

Inter vivos trust—A trust established by an individual during his or her lifetime, also known as a living trust. Such a trust can be either revocable or irrevocable. The opposite of a testamentary trust.

Irrevocable—A trust that cannot be changed after you've established it. This is an essential characteristic in order to have assets you give to the trust removed from your estate.

Issue—All descendants of a particular person. The term includes children, grandchildren and other direct descendants.

Joint tenancy with right of survivorship—Two or more persons holding title to a property jointly with equal rights during their lifetime with the survivor to receive the entire property. In other words, death of a joint owner automatically transfers ownership of the property to the surviving joint tenants. Joint tenancy will supercede any provisions contained in your will. Joint tenancy is different from tenancy in common.

Judgment creditor—A creditor who has obtained a court-ordered judgment against a debtor.

Judgment debtor—A debtor who has a court-ordered judgment against him.

Kiddie tax—Unearned income (dividends, rents, interest, and so forth) of a child under age 14. This income will be taxed to the child at the parent's highest tax rate. This tax makes family tax planning much harder.

Lack of marketability discount—One type of discount on the value of an asset. For example, the value of an asset given to a child may be less than its initial or expected value where, because of unusual circumstances, it is not readily salable.

Lease—A legal contract permitting one party to use property owned by another, usually for the payment of periodic rent. A common use of LLC's is to segregate valuable business assets (patent, trademark, real estate, equipment) in a separate entity, gift the interests in that entity to your children, and have them lease (or license) the right to use the property back to the business.

Liability—The condition of being responsible for possible or actual loss, penalty, evil, expense, or burden; the state of being bound or obliged by law or justice to do, pay, or make good something.

Limited liability—The characteristic of an entity that can be sued, but whose owners generally cannot be held personally liable for debts, or losses of the entity. The classic limited liability entity is the corporation.

Limited liability company, or LLC—An entity formed under your state's LLC statute that, like a corporation, has the legal characteristic of limited liability and that also may qualify to be treated for tax purposes as a partnership.

Limited partner—A partner (owner) in a limited partnership who contributes capital or property to the partnership but who cannot participate in the management of the partnership's business and who is not liable for partnership debts.

Limited partnership—A partnership with at least one general partner who has complete liability and control over the partnership and any number of limited partners with limited liability but no control or management over the business.

Liquidation—Termination and winding up of an entity, such as an LLC, corporation, revocable trust, etc. A final tax return will have to be filed with the IRS, and with state and local tax authorities. A tax clearance certificate may be necessary from the state. Usually a Certificate of Termination (or similar document) must be filed with the appropriate state agency.

Manager—The individual or entity charged with managing an LLC, making key decisions, and so forth. The Articles of Organization may specify who is to be the Manager. The operating agreement should provide details as to the scope of the powers of the Manager, liability for acts, replacement, and so forth. The Manager can be one individual, a group or committee of individuals, or even all members of the LLC. The

selection of the Manager can be important in determining whether the LLC has central-
ized management, which is an important characteristic in determining whether the LLC
can be taxed as a partnership or instead may have to be taxed as a corporation.

Marital deduction—An exemption from the estate tax for an unlimited amount of
assets that can be transferred from one spouse to the other. This approach is too often
used as the beginning and end of estate planning.

Member—With reference to limited liability companies, an owner of part (or in some
states all) of an LLC. A Member in an LLC is analogous to a shareholder in a corporation or a partner in a partnership. Some key characteristics and rights of a Member may
be set forth in the LLC's Articles of Organization. An Operating Agreement should be
drafted that specifically states a Member's rights, liability, and so forth.

Minority discount—A discount based on the concept that no person would pay as
much for a noncontrolling interest in an asset such as an LLC as for a controlling interest
(generally speaking, more than 50%). If you make a gift of an interest in you LLC to
your child, the value of the gift must be determined to ascertain whether a gift tax would
be due. The gift is generally valued at its fair market value. However, this value may be
reduced for a minority discount.

Operating agreement—The written contract between all the owners (Members) and
generally also those in charge of operating the LLC (Managers). An LLC Operating
Agreement is analogous to a corporation's shareholders' agreement and a partnership's
partnership agreement. This agreement should address in detail the rights and obligations of Members and Managers. It should contain buyout provisions in the event of the
death or disability of a member. Tax issues should be addressed: naming a Tax Matters
Partner and defining his or her rights; allocation f tax benefits; and so forth. It will
almost always be a mistake to think that an Operating Agreement can be avoided to save
costs.

Ordinary and necessary expense—With reference to taxes, a requirement for deductibility. For payments to be deductible, they must be ordinary and necessary expenses of
your trade or business. Extravagant or personal expenses will not be deductible. These
restrictions apply to your legal entities and this affect your ability as a member, partner,
owner, etc. to claim your share of deductions. Also, if asset protection is a concern, the
payment of personal expenses through most legal entities which grant asset protection,
in addition to tax problems, will increase the risk that the limited liability protection
afforded by the entities may be pierced.

Ordinary income—Income or gain from selling property that is not a capital asset. Ordinary income is taxed at rates of up to 39.6%, which is less favorable than capital gains rates of a maximum 28 %. There is an advantage for taxpayers to realize capital gains rather than ordinary income in many instances.

Organizational expenses—Costs incurred to set up a business, such as a LP, LLC, or corporation, that can't currently be deducted. Instead these costs can be written off (amortized) over 60 months beginning with the date your business, partnership, or corporation begins to conduct an active business. Be sure to discuss this with your accountant when organizing your legal entity.

Partnership—A syndicate, joint venture, group or other arrangement, in which two or more investors join their money and skills to carry out a business as coowners and to earn a profit. A partnership is generally treated as a flow-through (conduit) so that each partner reports his or her share of partnership income or loss on their personal tax return. The partnership files a form 1065 as an information report with the IRS but does not pay any tax. An election is available to avoid being taxed as a partnership.

Partnership interest—The ownership of part of a partnership. In addition to limited or general partnerships, since most LLC's are taxed as partnerships, your ownership of the LLC (your Membership interest) will be treated for tax purposes as a partnership interest.

Passive income—A type of income. The passive income and loss rules divide income into three types: (1) active (wages, income from and active business); (2) passive (income earned from rental property or as a limited partner investor); and (3) portfolio (dividends and interest on stocks and bonds). Passive losses (tax losses from rental property or from investments made as a limited partner) can only be applied to offset passive income. If you qualify as actively participating in a real estate rental activity, you may be able to deduct up to $25,000 of your passive tax losses against any income without regard to this limitation. Your interest in an LLC will be treated as generating passive or active income depending on the nature of the LLC's business and assets, as well as your involvement.

Passive loss—Tax losses from rental real estate properties (e.g., as a result of depreciation write-offs) or from investments as a limited partner. Passive losses can generally only be used to offset passive income.

Pass-through tax status—Profits that are not taxed on the company level but are distributed directly to members who report such profits as dividend income.

Personal property—Furniture, equipment, and other movable property and assets. Buildings and land are not personal property, they are real property. Real property and tangible personal property are generally subject to probate in the state in which they are located on your death. If you are domiciled (permanently reside) in another state, you can avoid ancillary probate in the state where personal or real property is located by transferring those tangible assets into a legal entity (such as a trust, corporation or an LLC) that may afford some estate planning benefits.

Pour-over will—As the name implies a pour-over will is used to transfer property to a living trust that was not transferred to the trust during the lifetime of the settlor. People often fund their living trusts with the majority of the assets that they own. However, any residual assets could be transferred to the trust after the settlor's death thorough the means of a pour-over will. All of the assets contained in the living trust prior to the settlor's death will escape probate. The assets poured over through the will will have to go through probate. The advantage of the pour-over will is that it provides for a uniform distribution of your property under the provisions of one single, legal instrument, namely the living trust.

Power of attorney—This is a legal document giving another person, known as agent or attorney in fact, the full legal authority to act in your behalf in your absence. A power of attorney loses its validity in the event the principal becomes disabled or dies. Most states, however, permit a durable power of attorney which remains valid through the disability or incompetency of the principal. A durable power of attorney can be used in conjunction with a living trust by allowing the agent to transfer any property that wasn't transferred prior to the disability of the settlor of the trust.

Present interest—A reference to a gift that the beneficiary can enjoy immediately. A gift must be of present interest to qualify for the annual $10,000 gift tax exclusion.

Probate—This is a judicial proceeding used for transferring a decedent's assets to his legal heirs. Its is a process of administering a deceased person's estate. Unless the estate is small, a will generally has to be probated. In the absence of a will the probate court appoints an administrator to handle the decedent's estate. All questions concerning the disposition and the rights of heirs and creditors are determined through probate. The actual probate process includes having the will recognized by the court (often called the Surrogate's Court), and having the person designated in the will (personal administrator or executor) officially empowered to act (often by issuance of documents called letters testamentary). Ancillary probate is probate in a state other than the state in which you reside. Ancillary probate, and the attendant fees and time delays can be avoided, in many instances, through the proper use of legal entities.

Probate guardianship—A judicial proceeding during which a guardian may be appointed by a probate court to manage the financial affairs of a disabled or incompetent person or of a minor. The guardian appointed by the court is required to make accounting of his actions to the court.

Pro rata share—A simple (from an economic perspective) LLC arrangement in which each Member shares pro rata in the income, expenses, profits and losses of the LLC. In a more complex arrangement, special allocations of income, expenses, profits, and losses may be used instead.

Registered agent—A person designated to receive notices directed to an entity. Most entities specify in the documents they file when formed a person upon whom notice should be given (served) in the event of a lawsuit or other matter. This designated person is often called a Registered Agent. If the person named moves to a new address, or is no longer appropriate (e.g. he or she is no longer associated with the entity), be careful to file the appropriate documents to change the Registered Agent and office.

Residuary—The assets remaining in your estate after all specific transfers of property are made and all expenses are paid. When a pour-over will is used, the residuary will be poured into your living trust.

Revocable trust—A trust that can be amended or terminated by its creator. As opposed to an irrevocable trust, a revocable trust generally has no tax consequences.

S Corporation—A corporation whose income is generally taxed only to its shareholders, thus avoiding a corporate level tax. An S corporation must meet numerous restrictions to qualify for this favorable tax treatment. An LLC is not subject to these restrictions and when structured to be taxed as a partnership (as most are) can have the same tax benefits of an S corporation with much greater ease and flexibility.

Section 2503(c) trust—A special trust established for minor children that permits gifts to it to qualify for the annual $10,000 gift tax exclusion even though they are not gifts of a present interest. Gifts of legal entity shares or interests can be made outright to a child or in trust for the child for even greater control. Where the gifts are made in trust, the 2503(c) rules can be important.

Securities—Stocks, bonds, notes, convertible debentures, warrants or other documents that represent a share in a company or a debt owed by a company or government entity.

Service business—A business that sells service or advice instead of a tangible product.

Shareholders—Owners of a corporation, may also be called stockholders. This is analogous to owners of an LLC, who are called Members.

Silent partner—A dormant or limited partner; one whose name does not appear in the firm and who takes no active part in the business, but who has an interest in the concern and shares the profits.

Sole proprietorships—A business run by one person that is owned and operated without any legal entity (no corporation, partnership, or LLC). Advantages of using a sole proprietorship are simplicity, no additional cost and one level of tax. The tremendous disadvantage is that the owner will have unlimited personal liability. An LLC is not an option for a sole proprietor in most states since at least two Members are generally required to form an LLC. The solution may be to make a spouse, child, partner, or business associate a nominal owner (Member).

State statutes—Laws created by a state legislature.

Tangible assets or property—Real or personal property; assets with physical value, as distinguished from intangible property.

Taxable income—Cash or certain economic benefits that you receive or have control over (constructive receipt), which are subject to tax (because no exclusion is allowed for them).

Tax basis—A formula for determining the taxable value of property. The amount invested to purchase property, plus the cost of capital improvements, less depreciation is the adjusted tax basis in that property. Your adjusted tax basis is the amount used to determine any taxable gain or loss on your sale of any asset.

Tenancy in common—A form of ownership of property by two or more persons. Different from joint ownership or joint tenancy. Upon the death of a tenant in common, ownership transfers to that person's heirs, not to the surviving owners.

Testamentary trust—A trust created in a will that does not come into existence until after the testator's death.

Testate—One who dies with a will.

Testator—The person who makes the will.

Trust—A legal entity in which a person or institution (trustee) holds or manages property for the benefit of someone else (beneficiary). The terms of the trust are generally governed by a contract that the grantor prepares when establishing the trust.

Trustee—An individual or institution holding and managing property for the benefit of someone else as per instructions contained in the trust agreement.

Unified credit—Permits and individual to gift (during life and death) up to $600,000 of assets to any person or persons without paying any federal estate or gift taxes on this amount. There have been many proposals to increase or decrease this amount.

Uniform Gifts (Transfers) to Minors Act (UGMA or UTMA)—A method to hold property for the benefit of another person, such as your child, which is similar to a trust, but which is governed by state law. It is simpler and much cheaper to establish and administer than a trust, but is far less flexible.

Uniform Limited Liability Company Act (ULLCA)—A uniform act proposed for LLC's. Many states have, or will eventually enact some version of this. Be careful not to assume that any particular state follows the ULLCA in all respects. There are often subtle, if not significant differences between the statutes in different states even were those statutes are based on the same uniform act.

Uniform Limited Partnership Act (ULPA)—A set of regulations for limited partnerships adopted by most of the 50 states, the District of Columbia, and several U.S. territories with some modifications.

Uniform Partnership Act (UPA)—A set of regulations for partnerships adopted by most of the 50 states, the District of Columbia, and several U.S. territories with some modifications.

Value—The worth attached to something exchanged. For purposes of making a gift of LLC interest or corporation stock, for example, you must determine the value of the interest or stock given away. For tax purposes, the fair market value is the value to use.

Will—A legal document that contains instructions for the disposal of a person or person's property under its prescribed terms upon said person or person's death.

Will contest—Litigation to overturn a decedent's will for lack of testamentary capacity, undue influence or lack of proper execution.